DATE DUE

Demco, Inc. 38-293

The Role of the Library in Distance Learning

**A study of postgraduate students,
course providers and librarians in the UK**

Also available in this series:

ELINOR Electronic Library Project
Anne Ramsden, Mel Collier, Clare Davies, Anil Sharma and Dian Zhao
Understanding Information Policy
Edited by Ian Rowlands
Effective Use of Health Care Information: A Review of Recent Research
Peter Merry
Quality Management and Benchmarking in the Information Sector: Results of Recent Research
Edited by John Brockman
Modernizing Research Libraries: The Effect of Recent Developments in University Libraries on the Research Process
Bob Erens
Information and Business Performance: A Study of Information Systems and Services in High Performing Companies
Ian Owens and Tom Wilson with Angela Abell
Electronic Publishing and Libraries. Planning for the Impact and Growth to 2003
Edited by David J. Brown
Project ELVYN: an Experiment in Electronic Journal Delivery. Facts, Figures and Findings
Edited by Fytton Rowland, Cliff McKnight and Jack Meadows
Networking in the Humanities
Edited by Stephanie Kenna and Seamus Ross
National Information Policies and Strategies: An Overview and Bibliographic Survey
Michael W. Hill
Changing Information Technologies: Research Challenges in the Economics of Information
Edited by Mary Feeney and Maureen Grieves
Teaching Information Skills: A Review of the Research and its Impact on Education
Edited by Rick Rogers
Decision Support Systems and Performance Assessment in Academic Libraries
Roy Adams, Ian Bloor, Mel Collier,
Marcus Meldrum and Suzanne Ward
Information Technology and the Research Process
Edited by Mary Feeney and Karen Merry
Information UK 2000
Edited by John Martyn, Peter Vickers and Mary Feeney
Scholarly Communication and Serials Prices
Edited by Karen Brookfield
Scholarship and Technology in the Humanities
Edited by May Katzen
Multimedia Information
Edited by Mary Feeney and Shirley Day

The Role of the Library In Distance Learning

A study of postgraduate students, course providers and librarians in the UK

Lorna Unwin, Kate Stephens
and Neil Bolton

London • Melbourne • Munich • New Providence, NJ

British Library Cataloguing in Publication Data
A catalogue record for this book is available from the British Library.

Library of Congress Cataloging-in-Publication Data
A catalog record for this book is available from the Library of Congress.

Published by Bowker-Saur
Maypole House, Maypole Road
East Grinstead, West Sussex RH19 1HU, UK
Tel +44 (0) 1342 330100   Fax: +44 (0) 1342 330191
E-mail: lis@bowker-saur.com
Internet Website: http://www.bowker-saur.com/service/

Bowker-Saur is part of REED BUSINESS INFORMATION LIMITED.

ISBN 1-85739-221-3

British Library Research and Innovation Report 96

Cover design by John Cole
Printed on acid-free paper
Printed and bound in Great Britain by Antony Rowe Ltd, Chippenham, Wiltshire

Contents

Acknowledgements

The research presented here was funded by a grant from the British Library Research and Innovation Centre (BLRIC) to whom we are very grateful.

We would like to thank all the students, course providers, university and public librarians who have helped us with this research. We are particularly indebted to Denise Harrison at Sheffield University Library for her unfailing support and to Biddy Fisher, formerly at the Library Association and now at Sheffield Hallam University, for her encouragement in the early phases of the project. The advice and guidance of Michael Hannon and Graham Bulpitt have been very much appreciated. We are grateful to everyone who attended the consultative conference held in Sheffield in April 1996. The conference provided important feedback on interim findings and contributed to the recommendations included in Chapter 7. Thanks also go to our Project Manager, Isobel Thompson of BLRIC and to Margaret Buxton, the project secretary, for her patience and hard work.

About the authors

Dr. Lorna Unwin is Director of the Centre for Research in Post-Compulsory Education and Training and a Senior Lecturer in the Division of Education, University of Sheffield. She and Professor Neil Bolton (now retired) were joint directors of the research project reported here. Kate Stephens worked as Research Assistant to the project and is now a Lecturer in Education at Sheffield.

Introduction

Over the last ten years, the number of distance learning (DL) programmes offered by UK universities has shown an enormous increase.
There is difficulty in obtaining accurate figures because of incomplete
statistical returns for DL which is often confounded with part-time
study. Our library survey shows, however, that over half of
conventional universities are currently involved in postgraduate DL
provision, with new courses planned in every subject area. As recently
as ten years ago such courses would have been rare, with DL confined
almost exclusively to the Open University and the University of
London External Degree Programme.

More and more 'traditional', campus-based universities have
moved towards provision of courses off-campus, either through fran-
chizing arrangements with colleges or through DL. The expansion has
occurred particularly in relation to postgraduate provision, since DL
with its arrangements for structured support for part-time learning is
likely to be an effective pedagogy for mature students who are in full-
time employment. Not only can such students, it is argued, study in
their own time and at their own pace, but their programme of study
can be related to their own work interests and professional development. Courses leading to Masters degrees for those in commerce and
industry and for teachers are particularly in evidence, although there
are many other professional needs now serviced through DL arrangements, for example in librarianship, law, social work, nursing, den-
tistry and others.

The very fact that DL students have, in general, no ready access to
campus facilities means that they present a different challenge to a
university provider than do on-campus students. Very little systematic
research, using survey or case-study methods to explore particular
issues, has been carried out.[1] Even in North America, where there has
been much recent interest in these issues, large-scale empirical re-

---

[1] This was apparent at an International Conference held at the University of Sheffield in
June 1995 at which delegates drew up a long list of basic research questions for
distance learning.

search projects have been rare, with many questions left unanswered. The present project arose out of the need to examine one major area: the use of the library by postgraduate DL students. There had been no large-scale and recent investigation of this issue in the UK until this study which began in September 1994. This study seems to be unique in terms of its geographical scope and consideration of a variety of stakeholder perspectives.

The major questions which formed the start of this study are:

- What are the experiences of students with regard to use of libraries on postgraduate DL programmes?
- What arrangements are course providers making for library use?
- How do university libraries perceive the role of the university library?
- In what ways and to what extent do public libraries support DL students?

Students, course providers, university librarians and public librarians are the major stakeholders in the business of supply and demand of library services. A satisfactory solution to students' library needs clearly requires that these stakeholders are aware of each other's capacities and perspectives. Course providers need to know how students experience their use of the library throughout their course; and they need to be aware of the role their own library can play, and of the support available from public libraries. University librarians need to know the practices and expectations of their own course providers; whilst students can reasonably expect to receive clear and explicit guidance and support. There is, in short, a large problem of coordination: within universities, between academic departments and the library; between course providers and their students; and between universities and public libraries. Moreover, since DL students often wish to use university libraries other than the one at which they are registered, there are issues of coordination at the national level—between universities—that need to be addressed in order to ensure that students are not disadvantaged. The importance of these matters is highlighted by recent developments in the assessment of teaching quality. Undoubtedly, many principles of quality assessment will apply equally to distance and full-time postgraduate students, but in the former case we would surmise that access to library facilities would be as significant for students and for the effectiveness of course delivery as adequate communications between tutor and student. We anticipate, therefore, that our study can make an important contribution to quality assessment procedures for a growing segment of the university population.

To repeat, it is through an investigation which is sensitive to the perspectives of the different stakeholders, we believe, that satisfactory answers can be provided with regard to effective library provision. We need to discover both what is required by our clients, the students, and what is possible within the constraints of institutional funding. There may, in fact, be a number of different ways in which progress can be made, depending perhaps mainly on the nature of the course and its requirements, but also on such factors as the different requirements and learning styles of students and the availability of resources. However, there are two underlying themes to which decisions about provision are likely to be referred, and it may be useful to signal these clearly now.

The first is that of learner autonomy. The effectiveness of DL is often predicated on the encouragement it provides for active, independent learning. This emphasis would appear particularly appropriate at the postgraduate level at which one would normally expect students to engage in literature searches and investigative work. But do course providers have an explicit and considered policy on the role they wish the library to play in fostering autonomous learners? There are, clearly, pedagogical issues entailed here which we see our research as commenting upon, for what course providers say, or fail to say, may have significant implications for their students' styles of learning.

The second theme is that of the place of information technology and telecommunications. The potential of electronic information access for radically altering the way learning takes place has been frequently commented upon (HEFCE, 1993) and idealized future scenarios have been sketched in which relevant and required information passes speedily between librarians, students, and course providers at the press of a button. We suspect that the present reality falls well short of this picture, and our investigation, particularly a diary study recording library use over a twelve month period, describes actual use of IT facilities. But there can be no doubt that DL provision will be more and more shaped by facilities made available by advancing technology—literature searches from a student's home or video-conferencing are cases in point—and course providers will need to take an educationally grounded view of what practices they wish to follow.

The present study: a note on our methodological approach

In order to explore the complex relationships which are created in the delivery of DL courses, we decided to adopt a multi-layered methodology involving the following methods: large-scale questionnaire surveys; semi-structured individual and group interviews; and student diaries. By collecting data using these different methods, we are able to present both a quantitative and a qualitative picture of the role of libraries in postgraduate distance learning in the UK. At every stage of the research, we have consulted with representatives from the key stakeholder groups: DL students; course providers; and university and public librarians. We have also been in close contact with the relevant professional bodies and government agencies concerning the policy context for DL and higher education (HE) in general. The rapid expansion of DL and the diverse range of subject disciplines now covered have meant that we have had to ensure we kept abreast of the changing context for our research. We were helped in this by a network of advisers actively involved in the design and delivery of DL, to whom we are very grateful for their support and constructive advice.

In carrying out a review of the literature on DL from the UK, North America and Australia (see Chapter 1), we discovered that, up until our study, there had not been any research which brought together the perspectives of the different DL stakeholders. We wanted, therefore, to design a methodology for our study which was broad enough to allow those perspectives to be given adequate space and parallel status. The quantitative element allowed us to collect statistical data related to numbers and types of DL courses, to construct a profile of DL students, and to ascertain the range of issues concerning university and public librarians. The qualitative element of the study provided us with a wealth of important data from students, course providers and librarians about their lived experiences of participating in distance learning. We were then able to compare and contrast those experiences and so create what we believe to be the first in-depth analysis of postgraduate distance learning from the perspective of the key stakeholders.

In April 1996, we invited representatives of the different stakeholder groups (DL students, university and public librarians, and course providers) and relevant professional associations to participate in a 24 hour seminar in Sheffield to discuss our interim findings. Some 60 people from throughout the UK attended. A report of our interim findings was circulated to delegates prior to the seminar which meant that, after a short introduction from the research team, delegates could respond to the different elements of the study. This event forms part of our overall methodological approach which deliberately set out to be as consultative and participatory as possible. Delegates at the seminar confirmed that our interim findings accurately reflected the problems and challenges posed by the growth of postgraduate distance learning, and highlighted the need for much closer cooperation between course providers and librarians in the design and delivery of DL courses. In addition, the delegates offered further insight into the issues raised by the research and this important supplementary evidence is presented as part of our concluding chapter (see Chapter 7).

The specific methodological approach adopted for these investigations is described at the beginning of the relevant chapters.

The research study consists of five related investigations conducted between September 1994 and September 1996 as follows:

- Completed questionnaires were returned from some 1,000 students in postgraduate DL students in the UK.
- Forty-seven of the students who completed the questionnaire kept a diary over a period ranging from 3 to 12 months in which they recorded their library use and experiences.
- Eleven course providers were interviewed with a view to eliciting their perceptions of the issues involved in library provision for their students.
- A questionnaire was distributed to 158 librarians at HEFC funded institutions; 116 completed questionnaires were returned.
- A sample of public libraries was approached, including branch or central libraries from all regions in the UK. Of these 138 were returned.

The chapters that follow describe these studies and outline the major findings. A review of the international literature is presented and a final chapter brings together the major trends identified and suggests further necessary developments both in research and in good practice.

CHAPTER 1

The role of the library in distance learning: a review of UK, North American and Australian literature

Extent of the literature

Much of the material discussed in this review has been obtained from a small number of important sources. Latham, Slade and Budnick published in 1991 an annotated bibliography with 535 references relating to library services for off-campus and distance education, which was intended to be comprehensive from the 1930s through to 1989, with some studies from 1990. In 1996, Slade and Kaskus published a further bibliography, which was originally planned as a supplement to the first but turned into another book, with 518 further references largely relating to work published in the intervening period, and including a few missed in the first survey. Both bibliographies are international in scope. Useful summaries of the literature for Canada, Australia and the UK are provided by Carty (1991) in an unpublished dissertation for an M.Lib. degree. Also in 1991, an issue of *Library Trends,* devoted to off-campus and DL provision, provided summaries of local situations in various countries by various authors referred to below. In addition, the proceedings of the various conferences for off-campus librarians held in North America since 1982, including the 7th and most recent conference in 1995, have been a useful source of information. With the notable exception of Burge's work in Canada, attention has come almost exclusively from within the librarianship profession. The field has been paid little attention by course providers and, while there is an undercurrent of dissatisfaction with this situation, librarians have rarely directed their research attention to investigation of the course provider perspective.

Note on terminology

The field of DL is fraught with terminological difficulties, perhaps not least because of its concern to dissociate itself from the negative associations of the correspondence course. In the UK the terms 'open learning' and 'flexible learning' both have currency, and the abbreviation ODL for open and distance learning is also used. The term 'open learning' has tended to signal notions of access and the expansion of higher education opportunities, often to non-traditional and part-time students; whereas the term 'flexible learning' has signalled a new customer orientation, and is attached to notions of self-paced study in connection with full-time employment. Flexible learning has also become attached to a particular response to undergraduate expansion: the development of structured self-study learning materials for full-time, on-campus students. Prior to the recent expansion of continuing education, the idea of the 'external student' was often associated with non-award bearing courses served by book boxes, that is small collections of material deposited at a convenient location for a particular course.

In the United States, the historical notion of the external student has given way to the term 'off-campus student'. Librarians' discussions of off-campus students seem to include both the serving of satellite colleges or extended campuses and the idea of DL in the sense of an individual home-based student studying from course materials at a distance from the institution. Often the two are not clearly distinguished, and it is sometimes difficult to tell from the literature which type of situation is being discussed.

In Canada, the use of the term 'distance learning', which is not associated with satellite or split-site or extended campuses, seems to be more common than in the US, although the provision of small deposit libraries at off-site locations still seems to be a common practice. The terms 'off-campus' and 'distance learning' are often used interchangeably.

According to Crocker (1991):

> In Australia, *external studies* is the term more widely used to describe those students who study with a university or college by correspondence, but, increasingly, 'distance education' and 'off-campus studies' are used interchangeably with external studies. (p. 496)

Partly because of lack of interest by academic course providers, and partly because of the fast pace of change, the field lacks a precise and defining typology. Indeed, the above terminological distinctions may have little meaning from the librarian's point of view. Because the literature, with very few exceptions, is generated from within the librarianship profession, it tends to be organized in accordance with conceptions of student library needs rather than course labels or structures.

For the purposes of this review, an inclusive approach to the literature has been adopted. Studies are discussed that refer to any of these associated terms, although an attempt has been made to distinguish where research or theoretical discussion has specific implications for DL, in the sense of home-based students studying individually from course material.

The United Kingdom

In the UK, the provision of library services to DL students has been a neglected subject for both empirical research and policy discussion. The early vision of the role of the public library service in meeting the needs of Open University (OU) students met with some disquiet regarding adequacy of stocks and funding. In 1969 Ashby, a senior librarian in the public library sector, described plans for the OU as a being like a Loch Ness Monster, only intermittently and partially available to the public view. Pointing out the already existing library subsidy for higher education provided by the public libraries, he predicted a new and specialized level of demand on the public library service:

> The degree to which the established universities rely on public libraries to produce the required books is little appreciated. Most public librarians know that they are giving valuable and unacknowledged support to both university students and staffs, and are meeting the demand for books which university libraries, for all their resources, do not seem able to cope with on the necessary scale. Yet universities are specifically equipped with all the apparatus of learning. How much more will the OU student, home-based and distant from Milton Keynes, turn to his local library as his university library, for books and for other facilities as well? (p.326)

With the OU about to open its doors the following year, Ashby voiced what he considered to be a widespread concern about the absence of a machinery for consultation in the planning stages of the new university:

> There is some dismay that no formal arrangements for direct consultation between the Open University and the Library Association at present exist. (p.327)

In 1971 Simpson, Librarian of the Open University, wrote apparently reassuringly of the demand to be made on public libraries for background reading material:

> In the latter part of 1969 it had been thought that this might cause heavy demands on local libraries. During 1970, as the writing of the courses progressed, it became clear that the amount of reading contained in the printed course units and in the set books was considerable, so that few students would have time for additional background reading. (p.168)

But in 1973, while recognizing that the provision of published readers might also be a time saving device for the first year undergraduate student in residential universities, Simpson emphasized that the demands must be different for higher level courses. Speaking of levels 3 and 4 OU courses, he said:

> Here the scene changes. In some of these courses the student cannot be fully served by Set Books and the printed Course Units. He needs to work actively with the literature of his subject and its bibliographical apparatus. He will not be able to buy all the essential books he needs and will have to seek some of them in local libraries. (p.175)

In the same paper Simpson reported a survey conducted in 1971 by the Open University's Institute for Educational Technology. Based on 977 responses to a Summer School questionnaire, it had been found that 69 per cent had obtained 1,647 background reading books between them, with 42 per cent borrowed from public libraries, 13 per cent from other libraries, 35 per cent bought and 10 per cent borrowed from other sources. He presented figures to show that, with 42,000 students in 1973, and with half of these taking lower level courses, and the remainder spread thinly over a large number of courses with relatively small overall numbers of students, the cost to the public library service per year per 1,000 population could be estimated at £1.20.

The debate over the role and cost of the public library service to DL students waned towards the end of the 1970s. Carty (1991) summarizes the arguments in a thorough but unpublished literature review of the comparative consideration of these issues in the UK, Canada and Australia. Her review concludes that provision of services was less than adequate in all three localities, but that:

> The UK Open University, as a mass provider of distance education, has chosen one method of dealing with the provision of access to library resources for its students—to relinquish responsibility to other libraries. (p.29)

Carty quotes a small number of user surveys conducted on OU students during the 1970s. In 1975, a survey of the use of libraries by OU students in the Yorkshire region (Masterson and Wilson, 1975) indicated a relatively low level of library use and suggested that use might increase with higher levels of study. This idea was tested out in a small survey reported in 1978. Based on 82 questionnaire responses from students in three regions, Wilson (1978) reported an increased use of library resources, especially for project based courses, with opening hours, travelling times and costs the most frequently cited obstacles to library use. The survey indicated the need for better preparation of students in the use of libraries as well as better local information on the availability of resources.

The library needs of postgraduate students was one of the subjects of an unpublished Open University internal report on the student's perspective in 1981 (Swift, 1981). The report, based on a survey of 271 of its own postgraduate students, found that students were using public libraries and university libraries to a similar extent (23 per cent and 25 per cent respectively), while 85 per cent found library arrangements 'fairly' or 'very' inadequate. A third of the sample identified time and travelling costs as major obstacles to library use, while 28 per cent identified borrowing rights as a major source of difficulty.

In 1984-5, Christine Crocker of Deakin University, an important voice in the promotion of DL services in Australia, conducted a study visit to the UK to investigate library support for extramural education (reported in Crocker, 1987 and 1988a). Her report refers to the virtual exclusion of extramural and part-time students from full academic library facilities due to off-site provision of book boxes and restricted library opening times. She cites with alarm the case of one university offering a part-time, on-campus evening degree course, serviced only by an extramural department book box. Her interest in the University of London postal loan system and external degree programme concluded that 'it would appear that the University of London Library has little contact with external students, and even less inclination to encourage their use of the postal library service' (Crocker, 1987, p.3).

Crocker also visited the OU in search of a model for library provision for DL students and librarian involvement in the preparation of course materials. She noted the high proportion of librarians' time spent on the clerical task of 'picture searching' for course materials and the still limited input to course development teams. While involvement in the production of library guides she noted as being a valuable development, she comments on the absence of any evaluation of their use or any 'comprehensive attempt to gather information on student use of libraries and resources'(Crocker, 1987, p.7). While noting that the role of the library may change over the next ten years, she writes:

> It is fair to say that I was disappointed in my perception of
> the Open University model of library liaison. (p.7)

Latham, Slade and Budnick (1991), who provide an international bibliography of the provision of off-campus library services, list seven user studies in the UK up to that date, with only two concerned with students of universities other than the OU. Of these, the most recent (Fisher and Bolton, 1989) was an evaluation of the University of Birmingham's book box system for extramural students and is based on questionnaire responses from approximately 966 of the University's own students. An earlier study of the number of Birmingham University book loans to extramural students had indicated that this group did as much reading as full-time students (Fisher, 1991). The two studies are relevant to the present study in so far as they point to the value and importance of library services for extramural students in general, but are not specifically concerned with the library needs of postgraduate DL students.

In 1991 Fisher's contribution to *Library Trends* reflects the then limitation of conventional universities' involvement in DL and also the imminence of change. The paper is part of a collection devoted to international developments in this field. Fisher reports a survey of higher education institutions which indicates the restriction of DL to the OU and the University of London, and predominant involvement of university extramural departments in education aimed at working adults. He indicated that the book box system, first developed in the 1920s, was then still the most important means of provision for these students. He points out the contradiction in the OU position on the use of libraries by its students. He suggests that reliance on the public library presents a 'major weakness in the system' (Fisher, 1991, p.490) for students who need to do wider reading beyond course material. The production of library guides and the incorporation of instruction in the use of libraries into course material are part of the OU's response to the charge of spoon feeding its students through reliance on provided material (Dale, 1982). But commenting on the provision of library guides by OU staff which indicate the vital importance of library use, Fisher points out:

> These guides are excellent for those students who have access to a good library, but they may add to the frustrations of those who do not. (Fisher, 1991, p.490)

In the following paragraph, Fisher predicts the change in course provision that was about to follow, and advocates a solution to the library access problem:

> The time is right for universities to move more positively into the provision of off-campus part-time degree and diploma courses. This should be predominantly by traditional face-to-face classroom teaching, partly because this is what conventional universities are best at, but also because the Open University already provides highly structured distance teaching. But this would require a firm commitment by universities to give proper library support. A start could be made now toward formulating such a commitment based on the existing work of extramural libraries and on new guidelines (as recommended above), but also involving closer coordination with the Open University and with the London University External Degree

Programme. This coordination should be concerned with course provision as well as library support, with the objective of reaching a national system to replace the present fragmentation. (p.492)

Since Fisher's research, huge changes have taken place in the provision of DL courses by conventional universities. Some progress has been made in the provision of services by certain institutions. For example, Sheffield Hallam University has a postal and literature service targeted at DL students and this has been the subject of a user survey indicating, from 200 questionnaire responses, a 50 per cent take up of special services with the vast majority of respondents expressing satisfaction with the services provided. Walker and Ward (1994) and Ward (1995) describe the service and plans for a further user survey of 800 students. Jolly (1995) describes similar service developments at Northern College in Scotland for approximately 1,000 teachers, social workers and community education workers studying for postgraduate degrees by DL. Special services are also provided by the University of the West of England and the University of Wales at Aberystwyth.

But the basic problems still remain. No progress has been made towards national reciprocal cooperation, and this seems unlikely in view of increased institutional competition and decreased resources. Students' levels of skill in the use of library resources may be an increasing problem. In 1994 Coles presented a paper to the Medical Health and Welfare Librarians' Annual Conference reporting the results of a small scale survey of students on a Masters course in Health Information Management and drawing on her own experience as both a librarian and a DL student. From the survey she describes the 'average' DL student:

> She was female and aged 38. She left full time education at 21 and worked in middle management or administrative post. (p.2)

She continues:

> It is likely that on leaving education students have never had to read an academic journal, in some cases they are quite unaware that textbooks and journals are fundamentally different in the type of information they supply.

A major problem for DL students is that they can arrive at
the library with a similar or lesser skill level than the new
undergraduates or nursing students but they do not benefit
from any organised induction sessions or instruction in
library use, and then are expected to produce work of
degree level or higher straight away. (p.3)

She goes on to point out the danger that too many assumptions may be
made about students' levels of skill because of the age and professional background of the people involved.

For the first time in the UK, Unwin (1994) surveyed postgraduate
DL students across institutions. In recognition of the increasing size
and variety of courses being offered by DL, Unwin surveyed 350
students at four UK universities. This study seems to have been the
first to attempt to look at the problem across the UK university sector
in the light of the recent postgraduate expansion and effectively
formed the pilot study for the present survey.

There has been some recent research interest in problems which
touch upon the concerns of the present study. For example, a recent
British Library funded investigation into library support for degree
courses franchized to further education institutions has indicated that
these arrangements have had little impact on the services provided by
university libraries (Goodall, 1994) and that there has been a low level
of involvement of FE librarians in course planning (Goodall, 1995).
While generally relevant to the pressure on library services and their
importance for study in general, this work is focused on the need of
full-time students being taught face-to-face on undergraduate courses.

The work of Allred (1992) on open learning and public libraries is
relevant only in so far as it is generally supportive of the needs of
adult learners. Allred surveyed 174 public libraries for the extent to
which they stocked open learning packs. The work is partly an
evaluation of the Employment Department's *Open for Learning* project which was intended to promote the provision of open and flexible
learning materials for adult learners. The initiative is not directed at
degree level study, and since it is concerned with the provision of
structured learning materials rather than wider reading opportunities,
it has very limited relevance to the present study.

Of greater potential relevance is the recent European Commission
(EC) funded investigation into the use of information technologies to
improve services to distance learners (the BIBDEL project). Three
demonstration projects at the Universities of Central Lancashire, the

Aegean and Dublin City are described by Wynne (1994). These are concerned respectively with: communications from an associate college with a subject librarian, the Online Public Access Catalogue (OPAC) and a range of networked CD-ROMs; telecommunication connections between four small libraries; and the use of email and modems to provide services to home-based students. In two reports (Wynne *et al.*, 1995a and 1995b) a variety of issues are discussed, including copyright, cost-effectiveness, user education and staff training. This work is of great relevance for its exploration of the potential of electronic communications to deliver the services users require. It should help to set in a more realistic context some of the more speculative writings about the so-called 'electronic library'.

However, the present study, described in this report, seems to be unique for its exploration of current practices in library use by post-graduate students. Its concern is mainly with the normal means of access which students have to library services, which currently remain, to an overwhelming extent, personal visits, supplemented by telephone calls and postal services. It should also give a perspective on the current extent of involvement with computer mediated net-worked communications, and librarians' views on the possibilities and limitations of these new technologies.

North America

The United States

In certain respects, interest in library services for DL, under the um-brella term of 'off-campus study', seems better established in North America than in the UK. Yet examination of the literature shows only a small number of empirical studies which go beyond user surveys at particular institutions and individual institutional case studies. Voices arguing for an educationally theorized case for library use based in extensive empirical research are rare.

Brophy (1992), in a report of a study visit to North America, notes the impact of distance on the delivery of education and library ser-vices. Generally the notion of off-campus study in the US refers to geographically dispersed campuses with delivery of courses face-to-face or by teleconferencing. Brophy reports that dedicated collections are a common feature of education delivered at dispersed campuses, with relative degrees of access to a central collection and postal ser-vices quite common. There are almost always some staff dedicated to off-campus delivery, although this may be only part of their duties and they may not be professionally qualified. Some kind of library skills training is usually attempted, although this is frequently of an introductory nature. He reports relatively little cooperation between libraries, even of the same type, and expresses concern about relatively low level of uptake due to the narrow content focus of many courses.

Concern about the library access needs of adult extension students in the US goes as far back as 1929. In a foreword to the *American Library Association Bulletin* of 1931, the library needs of extension students are firmly asserted:

> The student working by himself on a farm or in some small town, writing out his reports week after week and sending them to a university instructor, is often the most serious type of reader. He is, perhaps by virtue of the very difficulties he must overcome in order to study at all, a person of exceptional initiative and ambition and therefore most eager to read and most capable of profiting by the use of books.

> No history is properly taught by the means of one textbook, no course in literature can be adequately handled in one volume, no study of business problems is authoritatively set forth in its entirety by any one writer. And yet all too often, with books lying on the shelves of our university, state, and local libraries, the student has gone book hungry, and the instructor has had to make the best of a very bad educational situation. (ALA, 1931, p.675)

The report notes that only a few libraries had, as yet, accepted their responsibilities to such students. A questionnaire survey of library provision is reported with responses from 32 universities in the US. Wide variation in practice is noted by different states, with only a small number of universities either setting up local collections or delivering material directly to the student. The report notes the wide variation in public library facilities in urban areas compared to small towns and suggests that the burden of responsibility for easing the situation rests with the university sector.

Currently, the University of Michigan has one of the best services for off-campus students. Flanders (1956) gives some of the history of the service, which seems to have been first funded in 1916 with a sum of $1,000 per year to respond to requests for books from a variety of groups including external students. Referring to the future needs of the University's expanding extension programme, she notes:

> It will be difficult, however, for any but the very large public libraries to furnish the technical and special interest materials needed for some of these classes. Expanded staff and added book funds therefore will need to be provided as extension centres are added and class offerings are increased.
>
> One of the pressing needs of students registered in off-campus classes is for access to professional journals in education, sociology, psychology and social work. This is especially important for graduate students engaged in advanced work. Added book funds would allow this type of material to be made available in the extension centres. (p.168)

The University of Michigan currently plays a key role in the development of discussion in the field through the publication of a national directory of off-campus services and the organization of the regular off-campus librarian conferences (Jacob, 1991, 1993, 1995).

Latham *et al.* (1991) list 21 off-campus user studies in the US, while Slade and Kaskus (1996) list a further 12 references. These seem to be almost exclusively concerned with the evaluation of services offered by individual institutions, with comparisons between institutions or general questions of library access being only occasionally addressed. One exception is Groark (1974) who surveyed non-resident students at three universities which provided little or no library service. He noted that students use public libraries more frequently than those of their respective institutions and suggested that appropriate funding should be available from the universities. A further notable but unpublished survey conducted by Stasch (1994), sought to determine what sources of reading are used by students when the campus library is not available. She found that students tend to be influenced by convenience rather than content, and that while undergraduates are inclined to find material in academic libraries, home collections and bookstores, graduate students use academic libraries, home collections and workplace libraries. Women were more inclined to rely on their friends as sources of material than were men.

Despite the relatively well developed notion of off-campus provision in the US, and the existence of a bi-annual conference for off-campus librarians at which a large number of small scale and local user surveys are reported, there seems to have been little research of a large scale and systematic nature. The need for such research was emphasized by Slade (1995a), who is co-author of a Canadian library survey as well as two recent bibliographies of the field, at the most recent Off-Campus conference in San Diego, California. From a survey of 56 librarians attending the conference, he identified a number of research priorities. The top four were: bibliographic instruction; use of new technology; perceptions of campus administrators; and funding of services (Slade, 1995b).

Kaskus and Aguilar (1988) predicted the expansion of off-campus programmes in the US to redress declining enrolments of traditional students due to demographic changes. They identify the vital link between quality and course accreditation and the provision of library services as follows:

> Library support is an integral part of quality education and vital service which should be available to all students, whether on-campus or off-campus. (p.29)

They point out that the surge of interest in off-campus programmes began in the early 1970s in response to calls for the needs of a *learning society*. However, this expansion has led to some sharp emotional responses:

> Ironically, the proliferation of off-campus centers has become one of the most emotional issues in higher education . . . the issue of assuring quality education in off-campus programs has been a source of acrimony within the formal education system.

> Off-campus education is an idea that typically evokes biased attitudes and knee-jerk reactions. Faculty in general are opposed to the concept and have considered off-campus programs to be second rate. From the on-campus faculty perspective, off-campus programs are perceived to be of lesser importance; off-campus programs are per-

> ceived to be a threat; and off-campus students are per-
> ceived to be less serious. The failure of faculty to
> recognise the viability and potential of the off-campus
> student has contributed to the low status of off-campus
> programs and has prevented these programs from being
> fully integrated into the higher education mainstream. The
> issue of quality control will remain a major obstacle in the
> path toward recognition and full acceptance of off-campus
> programs as long as they remain outside the mainstream.
> (p.30)

They suggest that off-campus provision has presented a timely reminder of the importance of the library in academic study and that the current situation was one in which institutional solutions vary widely and range from 'total neglect to spoon-feeding'. They note problems associated with the size and scope of branch libraries and consider off-campus students to be 'at an academic and intellectual disadvantage in comparison with on-campus students'. The option of 'trunk delivery'—transporting materials by car—they consider inadequate because it does not 'provide access to the tools needed to perform even rudimentary research'. They call for a systematic approach to the solution of these problems and suggest a model for provision with three elements: use of the home library; a designated off-campus librarian; and agreements with non-affiliated libraries. They suggest that agreements with nearby libraries could include borrowing and access to bibliographical tools and instruction, for which libraries could be financially reimbursed. Many of these points are re-emphasized by Aguilar and Kaskus (1991) in their introduction to a volume of *Library Trends* devoted to off-campus provision.

In the same volume, LaBrake-Harrison (1991) discusses whether the Association of College and Research Libraries Guidelines for Extended Campus Library Services, published in 1981 and revised in 1990, should have been changed to national standards. She concludes, however, that the recently strengthened guidelines are a better interim solution than unrealistic standards. The issue of models of provision is taken up by Lessin (1991) who describes services provided by Webster University, University of Maine, Vermont State College, University of South Alabama and Central Michigan University. While the first four are described as having positive features, Michigan is considered to have the most comprehensive service in the light of the newly revised guidelines, and differs from all the others in its emphasis on making the main campus library the primary resource for all its students.

In the course of his study visit to North America, Brophy (1992) noted that off-campus librarianship seemed to be still a matter of peripheral concern enjoying low status in the librarianship community. This low status seems to be mirrored by the low status of off-campus programmes in the eyes of many teaching staff. In view of this, Kaskus's (1994) report of a study which gives an overview of what library schools teach about library support to distant students is timely. Her paper includes a review of the increasingly large literature on off-campus provision, which seems to mirror the expansion of programmes, but which does not seem to have been reflected in the curriculum of library education. Among the objectives of her study were: to gather baseline data regarding the place of this specialism on the curriculum; to investigate faculty attitudes towards its inclusion; and to identify individuals who might be interested in a curriculum development project. She approached 59 American Library Association (ALA) accredited programmes in the US and Canada, received responses from 39, and describes the findings as both discouraging and encouraging. On the one hand, no library school indicated the existence of a dedicated course, but 35.9 per cent said that the topic was included as part of another course. Only 18 per cent of course directors considered library support for such programmes to be adequate, and 59 per cent agreed that such courses tend to be taught differently because of the lack of such support. While only 20 per cent thought it would be possible to expand the curriculum to include a special course, 43.6 per cent indicated that existing courses could be modified to include the topic.

Canada

In comparison to the US, the Canadian situation is somewhat different. While in the US extended or satellite campus provision with face-to-face teaching seems more common than DL, in Canada, due to a more thinly dispersed population, the predominance of face-to-face teaching seems to be less pronounced. This difference is noted by Slade (1991) in a review article which gives an overview of the Canadian literature and also summarizes some of the findings of *The second Canadian off-campus library services survey* (Slade, 1988). This study was funded by the Canadian Library Association and was intended to extend and make comparison with some of the findings of an earlier Canadian survey (Slade and Webb, 1985).

The 1985 survey covered 42 Canadian university libraries, outside British Columbia, and identified 20, out of 31 replies received, as involved in the provision of services for off-campus and distance education students. Including British Columbia universities and the Open Learning Institute, 24 were identified as active in this kind of provision. Slade and Webb (1985) identify 13 components of a comprehensive library service:

- deposit of a core collection at an off-campus site;
- sending material in response to requests by phone or mail;
- answering reference queries and conducting subject searches in response to mail or telephone requests;
- offering a free telephone line to request material;
- advertising the existence of special services;
- at least one full or part-time librarian with responsibility for off-campus services;
- at least one full or part-time member of support staff with responsibility for off-campus services;
- provision of bibliographic instruction to off-campus students;
- online literature searches conducted for off-campus students;
- interlibrary loan requests initiated for off-campus students;
- all library services provided free of charge;
- needs assessment undertaken and used to plan service;
- off-campus services periodically reviewed and evaluated.

While a large number of libraries were identified as having some level of involvement with the above services, this early study does not appear to evaluate degrees of involvement or levels of response to user requests. Inspection of the data presented suggests that, while 19 universities were at that time willing to respond to telephone and mail requests by post, five of these did not advertise the service and seven did not claim to offer such a service free of charge. Only 10 had either a full-time or part-time librarian responsible for such services, and one university seems to have been included as 'active' only on the grounds of supplying a core deposit collection at an off-campus site and not charging for the service (Slade and Webb, 1885, p.6).

The second survey (Slade, 1988) is much more extensive, attempting to cover the whole of the post-secondary sector in Canada.

It presents some complex calculations, leading to a league table of off-campus and DL provision which takes into account degrees of involvement and numbers of students served. This second survey covered 55 universities and 144 colleges and technical institutes, with response rates of 78 per cent and 53 per cent respectively. As well as investigating services provided, it also attempted to measure the amount of involvement with off-campus and DL provision. Some measure of involvement was reported by 86 per cent of the universities and 60 per cent of the colleges which responded. Of those which were involved with this type of educational delivery, 95 per cent of the universities and 85 per cent of the colleges are reported as providing some level of library support, in this case defined by at least one 'yes' answer to 15 questions regarding different aspects of support, including additional questions over the first survey which addressed the issue of consultation with teaching departments.

Questions were asked concerning numbers of courses and average enrolments at both undergraduate and postgraduate levels and for both colleges and universities. Of the universities who responded to the questionnaire, 18 reported involvement in face-to-face off-campus teaching at graduate level, and five with DL at the same level. The numbers of such courses reported ranged from one to 56 for off-campus teaching and one to 13 for DL. The average numbers reported were 11 and three respectively. These figures are rather small in comparison to undergraduate provision, with 26 institutions reporting off-campus teaching and 22 DL. Numbers of such courses reached 194 for a single institution (average 59) in the case of off-campus teaching and 180 (average 47) for DL. Distance learning seems to have been the less common mode in 1988, with relatively small numbers of postgraduate students.

Comparing the results of the 1988 survey to the 1985 survey, Slade reports that nine universities had increased their level of support, while five had decreased their level of support. Comparing levels of support with size of programmes, Slade concludes that:

> This data implies that the size of an institution's off-campus program does not significantly alter the level of library support which an institution is prepared to provide. (Slade, 1988, p72)

In other words, institutions with very extensive off-campus pro-grammes may not be offering significantly better levels of service than those with relatively few such courses.

In an attempt to compare institutions for the level of actual support they provide, as distinct from expressions of willingness to provide support, Slade has developed the 'off-campus library services index'. Using this method, the highest index scores are reported for Athabasca University and the University of Victoria, with the Univer-sities of British Columbia and Manitoba, and the Open University of British Columbia occupying the next three places in the league table (Slade, 1988, p.99). Institutions offering only a deposit off-site col-lection score the lowest. Slade notes that core or deposit collections, and the sending of specific items to individual students are the most common means of supporting off-campus students, with the majority of institutions claiming to offer both.

He also notes the particular importance of outreach services for geographically dispersed DL students. He defines these as existing where an institution advertises that it will send specific items to indi-vidual students and will conduct literature searches on request. On this definition, 71 per cent of universities which have some level of off-campus support offer an outreach service. Slade presents these data alongside levels of distance education provision. Inspection of the table shows that of the 22 universities offering distance education courses, four do not offer an outreach service, while the remainder do offer such a service.

Slade notes the low level of involvement of librarians in curricu-lum development for off-campus provision as well as the relatively low level of involvement in needs assessment. Less than half of uni-versities, and an even smaller proportion of colleges confirmed that the service was financed through a designated budget. He concludes:

> . . . the planning process for off-campus library services in Canada is relatively underdeveloped. The ACRL Guide-lines for Extended Campus Library Services (Assoc. for 1982) stress Planning and Finances as important in this area of librarianship. . . . The assumption underlying the issue of planning in this context is that effective off-campus library support cannot be provided on an ad hoc basis. To enhance the quality of off-campus programs, an institution has to recognise the need for non-traditional approaches to library services and establish mechanisms

to anticipate and control the demand for material. It is apparent that Canadian Universities and colleges are, for the most part, not actively involved in this anticipating and controlling process. (Slade, 1988, p.110)

He goes on to note that data about volume of business were only patchily reported in the survey returns and infers that *ad hoc* and unmonitored provision is probably very common. From the limited data available, Slade has calculated an 'item/student' ratio which gives an estimate of the amount of support supplied per student. The data show that while a high proportion of institutions claim to have an outreach service, many have a low level of business. This is particularly so for colleges, with only 15 per cent supplying one or more items per student on average, and 65 per cent supplying an average of 0.24 items or fewer. For universities, 30 per cent supply one or more items, with 37 per cent supplying 0.24 items or fewer. He concludes that accurate enrolment data are needed to get a more accurate picture of levels of involvement.

He suggests that there are three key questions which a future survey should ask:

(1) Are off-campus students encouraged or required to use library material in their courses?

(2) If yes, are students encouraged to use local resources or the 'home' library?

(3) If students are encouraged to request material from the 'home' library, are there sufficient resources and staff to assist the students? (Slade, 1988, p.114)

While these surveys may show relatively high levels of interest in off-campus provision compared to the UK, Slade appears less than satisfied with the Canadian situation. This sense of problems being inadequately addressed comes across more critically in his review article (Slade, 1991) in which he describes the growth of DL and off-campus provision, while noting the lack of research and the silence of the continuing education and DL literature on the provision of library services. In his 1996 bibliography, his annotation for Holmberg's *Theory and practice of distance education* begins as follows:

This work is cited because, to date, it is the only scholarly book on distance education to mention the role of library services. The references to libraries are brief and appear on four pages of the book. . . . (p.22)

Low level of use of libraries by students is of particular concern to Slade. He summarizes the surveys that have been reported as follows:

Emerging from the results of these surveys is a composite profile of the off-campus student in Canada. The average student is mature, female, often married, with a full-time job. This student tends to take off-campus courses for work-related reasons. Many of these students are able to complete their courses without the need of additional resources, and therefore, overall library use is low. Supplemental information is acquired directly from the course tutor . . . or through the purchase of books . . . When library materials are needed, students tend to turn first to their local public library. When students live within reasonable commuting distance of the campus library, there is a preference to use these facilities directly. For students further away from campus, there is a preference for having a core collection deposited in a local library. Common problems faced by these students are: distance from libraries, limited access hours, availability of appropriate materials, restrictive loan periods, difficulties with renewal of material, and 'time pressures'. (Slade, 1991, p.461)

Despite an increase in the volume of literature on the topic since 1985, Slade notes that only a small number of Canadian publications are reporting research data. He particularly cites the research by Burge, Snow and Howard (1988 and 1989) which he describes as the first Canadian work to propose a model of service provision based on original research.

While Burge *et al.* confined their study to Northern Ontario, it was more extensive than others for its attention to the various partners in the distance education process. It seems to have been unique in North America for its attention to relationships between educators, students and libraries and for its setting of an empirical survey within a theoretical discussion of the education process. Although a single questionnaire was initially intended for the research it quickly became evident that four separate surveys would be required for public librarians, academic librarians, faculty/instructors and students. Questionnaires were distributed in both English and French to all members of each constituent group in the region—1,750 questionnaires in all. Questionnaire data were supplemented by interviews with academic and public librarians.

Burge (1988) had proposed a learner-centred approach to DL which goes beyond Knowles's (1985) concept of andragogy. She proposes a 'neo-andragogical' model which does not assume that adults are self-directed learners. Instead, recognizing and respecting the realities and varieties of adult life-experience, such a concept would facilitate the interdependence of learners and the collaboration of educators. She considers that the question of how far DL design is truly learner-centred has been little discussed in the literature, and she proposes a set of guidelines for distance educators which, she claims, can assist 'a distance adult educator caught between a personal philosophical acceptance of a learner-centred view and the prevalence of highly directive, transmittal modes of distance education and teaching' (p.13).

While Burge's consideration of the issues in this paper is not specifically concerned with relationships to the library, it sets the context for her later consideration of the importance of library issues.

Her report of the Ontario library study discussed above is summarized in her opening keynote address to the 1991 Off-Campus Library Service Conference. (Burge, 1991) In this address, and drawing on her experience in librarianship as well as adult and distance education, she sets the findings within the context of a learner-centred approach to adult education which stresses both relationships and responsibilities in the learning process. While survey returns from academic librarians reported that 14 institutions currently supplied library services to DL students, concern was expressed by almost all about low levels of use by students because of lack of awareness of services, as well as either the belief or the reality that students can get by without using a library. The student responses indicated they received a large quantity of course material, with 67 per cent indicating that they received all the material they needed in order to complete their courses, with 'a significant number' indicating that they did not use libraries at all.

The study concludes that there is a process of exclusion for DL students that takes place under one or more of the following conditions:

- inadequate or no intra-institutional communication between library and distance staff;
- 'one-shot' orientation-to-library approaches to students;
- course designers who build library-based services out of courses;
- library staff who lack the knowledge of basic educational theory that would otherwise allow them to build partnerships with course designers and tutors, based on the use of some common language about how adults learn;
- students who are totally invisible or anonymous to library staff—not seen, not talked with, not written to;
- library staff who lack incentives and rewards to push themselves and their services beyond the familiarity and comfort of traditional routines;
- educators who adopt the transmission model of teaching ('give 'em fish') and who do not expect students to develop their own 'fishing rods'. (Burge *et al.*, 1989, p.333)

Burge and her colleagues focus upon the relationship between the various stakeholders in distance education in their report of the research. The following quotation illustrates their view of the problematic nature of many of these relationships:

Relationships between library staff and their peers, and between learners and their distance education colleagues drew comments ranging from the poignant to the poisonous.

While academic librarians felt they enjoyed from 'good' to 'excellent' relationships with public library staff, the feeling was not always reciprocated by the public library staff interviewed. Academic librarians, on the other hand claimed little success in relationships with faculty and distance education administrators. Terms such as 'poor', 'embryonic', 'distant' and 'minimal' were used to characterise present conditions, caused, it seems, by the fact that library staff are not included in distance education planning or processes to any great degree, and when called upon, are forced to 'react at the eleventh hour'. (Burge *et al.*, 1989, p.332)

They recommend that library services should respond to the expansion of non-traditional educational opportunities, and point out the need for training of librarians and the development of conceptual models for off-campus provision, which they consider to have been so far lacking. They present a seven point model, and consider that the challenge will be the extent to which library staff and educators can work together to integrate its various features, which are:

- programme and course planning;
- services marketing;
- resource development;
- data access;
- technical communications;
- services and materials delivery;
- professional development.

Key to course planning are the assigning of responsibility for such services to one staff member and an annual mechanism for transfer of information between the library and distance education administration. They also suggest a formula-based strategy for public libraries serving distance education students, which would allow the development of collections and the provision of physical space. Public library services could be marketed by notices indicating 'Distance Education is Spoken Here'. Electronic access to academic libraries should be facilitated through the provision of networked computer terminals at public libraries. Toll-free 24 hour answering machines should be installed in all academic libraries and both public and academic libraries should be equipped with fax machines. They propose consideration of a postal subsidy for educational providers. They stress the need for face-to-face and computer conference communication between academic and public library staff and propose the development of a fund to support innovative activity in the field.

In comparison to the UK coverage, the North American literature can provide some inspiration. The notion of off-campus library services is well established, in the context of a geographically dispersed population, and an historical concern for the needs of the adult extension student is evident. However, in the US off-campus provision seems to be more commonly concerned with the provision of core or restricted collections at satellite sites, with only the University of Michigan aiming for access to a main library collection. While concern about the accreditation of courses and the relevance of library provision to issues of quality assurance arose earliest in the US, where guidelines for such provision have been recently updated, it is in Canada that substantial empirical research and theoretical consideration of educational issues have taken place. This literature suggests an inadequacy of provision and use of library services, and an alarming absence of consideration of these issues from the course provider perspective. In 1991 Slade noted the absence of external pressure on Canadian institutions to meet the concerns of accrediting agencies or licensing boards, compared to the US. In 1993, the Canadian Library Association published its own guidelines.

The work of researchers such as Burge and Slade in Canada has led Carty to conclude, that while library provision in Canada is inadequate, it is forward looking in its concern to build a comprehensive service (Carty, 1991, p.55). Yet the situation in Canada seems to present serious cause for concern. One has the impression of librarians pressed into a defensive mode by both developments in information technology and the development of self-contained courses which seem to write the library out of the educational picture. Librarians seem to be torn between the desire to assert the value of current practice in the provision of off-campus services, thereby enhancing the status of their work, and their sense that there is a tidal drift in educational provision which is tending to dismiss and devalue the importance of library use for a key and growing group of students. With 67 per cent of students claiming to receive all necessary course material without recourse to a library, and librarians and their professional concerns excluded from the course development process, the situation does not look conducive to the kind of educational process outlined by Burge (1988).

Australia

As in North America, Australian librarians have increasingly addressed the issue of off-campus services over the last decade in response to the marketization of adult continuing education. According to Crocker (1991), in her review of the history of such services, Australia was one of the first countries to develop large scale correspondence education in response to the special problems presented by a dispersed population, and that:

> While one university has been providing distance education since 1911, the real push for off-campus students began in the 1970s. By 1988, forty-two colleges and six universities in Australia were offering external courses to almost 48,000 students. (p.495)

She reviews the various official reports which have led to the expansion of distance education, including a 1988 government report on higher education which announced the long term strategy to rationalize distance education through a commitment to fewer and larger institutions, created by amalgamating and consolidating current provision. Six Distance Education Centres were to be funded to develop off-campus courses within a framework of cooperation aimed at producing greater efficiency and quality. She notes that enrolments are grouped heavily in humanities, social sciences, education, business, commerce and economics, with a lesser number in science, of which the majority study computing science. She quotes a study by Anwyl *et al.* (1987) which shows that:

> . . .external students are predominantly mature in age—i.e., they are more likely to be married, to have children, and to be employed than their on-campus counterparts (p166). Most of them have average to above average incomes from professional jobs, and most already have tertiary qualifications. In order of importance, reasons for studying externally were found to be employment, distance, and the freedom offered by the external mode of study. In terms of their personal development during their studies, external students report that they have higher self-esteem, greater academic and intellectual interests; they also consider that they have much better communication and leadership skills as well as much better academic abilities; they feel a greater satisfaction with life in general (p167). (Anwyl *et al.*, 1987, quoted in Crocker, 1991)

She goes on to note that:

> Reports such as this have helped to dispel the aura of
> 'second class citizenship' that once hung over off-campus
> studies and those that taught in this mode. (Crocker, 1991,
> p.500)

Concern about the quality of distance education in relation to
library provision was expressed by Allen (1982). He speaks in force-
ful terms about the role of the library in traditional education and the
need to regard librarians as integral to the course planning process. He
notes that Australia has not followed the UK Open University in
failing to provide its own library services, partly because of the geographical sparseness of library resources. He notes, however, that the
commercialization of distance education in Australia is very much in
the OU model, and describes the expansion of distance education as 'a
minor intellectual gold rush'. He is concerned about the lack of educational thinking and planning that seems to have gone into this
expansion:

> Rarely in the arguments for, or through the development
> of, externalised courses has much been heard about the
> fundamental characteristics of higher education. At best
> there seems to have been a tacit assumption that an insti-
> tution established within the old university or the new ad-
> vanced education systems will intrinsically display those
> qualities in its courses about which many brave words
> have been penned, and that where such an institution
> enters the external studies field, its ideals and quality
> control mechanisms will apply. In fact, the externalisation
> process has all too often been an unthinking exercise in-
> volving the minimum of modification to an existing inter-
> nal course, leading frequently to impossible demands
> upon external students and upon the supporting services
> and resources of the institution. This situation is one in
> which libraries may be placed without any prior consulta-
> tion and without any or adequate provision to meet the
> unknown, unspecified and unassessed needs of students.
> (p.533)

Allen goes on to elaborate the centrality of the role of libraries in universities, in particular in developing the kind of critical attitude which will enable students to extend their learning outside the formal framework. He proposes a library-centred educational philosophy in which a programme of reader education will be central.

Maticka (1992), writing in an edited collection of papers entitled *Australian tertiary libraries: issues for the 1990s*, notes the special importance of distance education in Australia. She notes that all Australian universities provide some library services for their students and that these have improved in recent years. However, she asserts that this is due to the lack of any alternative because of the absence of an adequate public library system, rather than strong educational reasons. She notes the importance of DESIG (the Distance Education Special Interest Group within the Australian Library Association) in drawing attention to the needs of these students.

Maticka expresses disappointment at the failure of attempts to develop a reciprocal borrowing system, due partly to the belief of the old established universities that libraries should look after their own students. She notes developments in new technology which have allowed Internet access to library catalogues, as well as the technical possibility of requesting and receiving material online. However, she also notes that the promise of these new technologies should be seen in relation to the need for hardware investment as well as problems of licensing software and CD-ROMs.

Commenting on the expansion of Australian DL overseas, Maticka suggests that the commercialization of distance education will bring its own problems:

> These developments present special challenges for the libraries of distance education institutions. Open learning and continuing education courses are frequently marketed at 'nontraditional' students, who are not, for a variety of personal and educational reasons, interested in enrolling in traditional award courses. Their expectations of, and experience with library services, may be quite different from those of mainstream students. As they are paying considerable amounts for courses, these students could well be more demanding and have higher expectations of service, while at the same time may be less skilled in exploiting those services when offered. Students resident in other countries will frequently have a different experience

of libraries than have their Australian counterparts, a difference which will be compounded by physical distance;
the cost of sending material by air mail or international
facsimile could be considerable. (p.63-4)

She goes on to tackle the question of funding:

The issue of funding is particularly relevant; academic
staff who have successfully mounted courses for which
fees are charged tend to guard this income closely. The
principle that a percentage of this income should be used
to fund library services for the students involved has not
been generally accepted, but must be. (p.64)

Maticka is discouraged by the lack of concern about library services shown in the process for assessing applications for Distance
Education Centre status, and is concerned that a change in government policy away from the idea of restriction of the number of Distance Education Centres will make matters worse. She is particularly
worried by 'the assumption in some quarters that teaching units can be
self-sufficient' and notes one university offering courses which are
advertised as including such comprehensive material that the student
will incur no additional costs for library services. She asserts the
importance of the involvement of librarians in DL development in
order to instil in students the importance of libraries in lifelong learning. Clearly concerned about an apparent trend towards the exclusion
of libraries, she concludes:

In the midst of these uncertainties, the need for librarians
to assert, and demonstrate, the central role of libraries in
tertiary education has never been greater. (p.65)

While the Australian Library Association had discussed off-
campus services in 1972 and 1979, Store (1981) provided the first
survey on library services to external students. The survey covered 36
institutions and indicated a wide variation in the services provided.
Crocker summarizes the findings as follows:

While in some cases these variations may have reflected
the different models of external teaching, it was clear that
library services to off-campus students had been neglected

by some institutions. At the time of Store's survey, eight institutions provided completely separate external studies collections; fifteen integrated resources for external students into their main collections; four had a separate external studies collection as well as regional study center collections; while four had no separate library resources for external students. Other library services also varied from two institutions providing only a lending service, to those offering a considerable range of reference and other services to their external students. (Crocker, 1991, p.501)

She reports a further study, carried out by Bundy (1988) which reported considerable progress in many areas, but found that library use was still limited because of the lack of free telephone access, free return delivery of materials and access to online catalogues.

Having noted in her earlier review (1987) her disappointment in the search for a model for provision in the UK, Crocker notes her impression of the limited nature of improvements in support in Australia since that date:

> While there has been some development in access to on-line catalogs through advancements in automated library systems and networks, only a handful of libraries are providing toll free telephone access for their external students; even fewer pay the delivery charges both ways for material sent on loan. (Crocker, 1991, p.501)

While Store's (1981) impression had been that the Australian situation compared favourably to that offered in other countries, inspection of data quoted from Bundy's survey shows that only two out of 18 institutions pay delivery charges both ways, and two institutions appear not to lend material at all to external students. Crocker goes on to speculate that the rationalization of Distance Education Centres may improve possibilities for collaboration on improved delivery methods.

While Latham *et al.* (1991) and Slade and Kaskus (1996) included a total of 32 references to user studies in Australia, these seem to have been largely focused on the services provided from specific institutions and limited in scope. By comparison, a study by Winter and Cameron (1983) is highlighted by both Crocker (1991) and Carty (1991) in their reviews of the literature.

This study seems to have been the most extensive piece of research into distance learners' use of libraries in Australia, and has played a key role in the promotion of policy discussion in this area. The survey approached 2,000 students from 10 institutions and achieved a response rate of 73.5 per cent. Carty reports their finding that 25-27 per cent of students make use of the delivery services provided by their parent institutions, with this group and other students making use of other sources such as public, other academic, school and workplace libraries. Personal collections and public libraries were the most frequently used sources, with the most heavily used resources not always being the most highly regarded. Crocker also concludes from the survey that:

> A majority of off-campus students make very little use of the range of delivery, loan, and information services available to them.. . . Students responding to the questionnaire . . . strongly indicated that, no matter how good the service from the home institution, they prefer to consult library resources themselves at any convenient library. In doing this they can browse available books, determine their relevance to the study topic, and have immediate access to appropriate titles. (Crocker, 1991, p.504)

A further notable finding is that students who receive readers as part of their course material seem to make greater use of libraries to obtain further reference material than those who do not receive readers. Among the difficulties cited regarding the use of libraries were: short loan periods; insufficient copies of recommended books; cost of returns; and knowing what was available in the library.

The Winter and Cameron report also indicated that, overwhelmingly, students believe that the library service is an important part of their study (94.6 per cent). Yet 77 per cent felt that off-campus students were disadvantaged compared to on-campus students. Out of 60 per cent responding to an open-ended question for additional comments, almost one third wanted access to and borrowing rights at nearby institutions.

The finding that students made heavy use of public libraries has been confirmed by a survey of 1,195 Deakin University external students (response rate 56.2 per cent). Grosser and Bagnell (1989) confirmed that these students use public libraries more than any other type of library. They also note that 74.5 per cent of respondents lived within 5 kms of a public library. They use this evidence to support an argument for improved funding of the public library service, whose role in Australia is generally perceived as providing leisure reading only.

These findings led to the consideration of the idea of a national library card for external students. In 1986, the Commonwealth Tertiary Education Commission funded a survey of academic libraries which aimed to map current regulations on visiting borrowers and solicit attitudes regarding more open borrowing. The results are reported by Crocker, Cameron and Farish (1987) and Crocker (1988b). They describe the overall situation as 'variable and confusing' (Crocker *et al.*, 1987, p.9) with criteria for membership varying between individual libraries and regions. They note that:

> The paperwork is variable and often time consuming, and there are potentially long delays between the student's first enquiry and his registration as a borrower. (p.9)

The report notes that most libraries would find acceptable an appropriate standard card to identify students of other institutions, but there seemed to be little resolution regarding the source of the cost of administering such a system or the cost of lending to external borrowers.

Crocker (1991) later concluded that 'while a standard nationally acceptable library card was not necessary, standardized information, procedures, and undertakings were' (p.505)

A further study is reported by Harris (1989). She describes a survey of external library users which was conducted by interviewing visitors to the libraries of one university. Four hundred and thirteen questionnaires were completed over a 10 week period. She concludes that external use at current levels does not appear to disadvantage institutional users, but that the common perception that external users may put disproportionate demands on information services, due to their relative unfamiliarity with library systems, may be justified. She suggests that a key issue is how best to provide user education for external students.

In response to the discussion about reciprocal borrowing, Deakin University took over the compilation of an annual list of borrowing conditions for each state and for all Australia. Crocker (1991) concludes that since the 1986 survey, the situation remains variable and confusing and that:

> A problem free system for extending borrowing privileges
> to visiting student borrowers is needed; a system which is
> simple for the students so that it encourages them to reg-
> ister for loans, and is also simple for the libraries so that
> they can provide information to students and statistics to
> each other. (p.506)

In 1982 the Australian Library Association had published guidelines for library services to external students (Crocker, 1982). Crocker
(1991, p.504) reports a 1985 survey, which indicated that eight libraries had then evaluated their services and four introduced changes.
She notes some 'tentative discussion about the possibility of preparing
standards for this area of librarianship' and regards the rationalization
of distance education providers as an opportunity to develop such
standards.
She concludes:

> The development of external studies in Australia occurred
> so rapidly in the 1970s and 1980s that librarians were
> often forced to be reactive rather than proactive in the de-
> velopment of library services. With the government's new
> rationale for higher education in Australia, there is, for the
> first time, a national focus on cooperation and rationaliza-
> tion that will foster discussion and collaborative ventures
> between the libraries of the designated distance education
> centers . . . The future is an exciting one, where at last a
> united library voice may have a chance to provide quality
> library services to off-campus students. (p.508-9)

In conclusion, discussion about the use of libraries by DL students
has been more extensive in Australia than in the UK, with a greater
polemical concern in the 1980s about distance education expansion
and quality issues relating to library provision. However, while the
Australian literature may appear comparatively extensive, only a small
number of research studies go beyond the services or students of a
single institution. There do not seem to have been any Australian
studies that use research evidence to interrelate the perspectives of the
various stakeholders in distance education. While many allude to
course provider perspectives on library use, since Haworth (1982)
there seem to have been no studies which look at provider

perspectives in a systematic way. She had been unable to find any previously published study of teaching staff expectations of library use by their students. From 30 structured interviews with lecturing staff, she concluded that 'teaching staff need education in the ways in which more profitable use can be made by their external students of the library's collection' (p.160).

Conclusions

An underlying trend of marketization of distance education to provide for the needs of adult continuing education seems to be common to all the regions discussed, and this trend has led to a greater concern for the library use and needs of such students. Policy and polemical discussion have been greater in the US, Canada and Australia, where the development of DL across the university sector seems to have taken place earlier. Voices from within the professional associations of librarians have been more widely heard in North America and Australia perhaps because of the apparently relatively better situation in the UK regarding public library provision, as well as the tradition of public access to university libraries. This situation seems to have led to some complacency regarding the practice of the UK Open University, which has recently been challenged by public library cuts and the involvement of traditional universities in DL. The Open University, whose postgraduate expansion has also been significant, has responded by reviewing the role of its library and the promotion of electronic access to library resources.

A number of common themes emerge when the international literature is compared:

- Problems of library access are being inadequately addressed.
- There is concern in all areas that students are not making sufficient use of even those services that are available to them.
- There is an apparent trend towards the further exclusion of the library, against the background of librarians being already inadequately involved in course and curriculum planning.
- In the UK, North America and Australia, the reliance of students on public library services emerges as an issue. Despite apparently relatively poor levels of provision, North American and Australian students make at least as extensive use of the public library service as they do of those of the parent institution.

- The profile of the type of student served by the recent expansion is the same. Because students are mature and inexperienced in the use of modern library resources, they are in greater need of bibliographic instruction or user education than students who have traditionally been served by university libraries.
- There is a significant lack of detailed elaborations of educational perspectives on the role of the library in DL, or attempts to map the course provider's view through research.

The international expansion of adult continuing education through DL undoubtedly draws upon a vast pool of public and professional goodwill in relation to the self-supported and independent adult learner. It is ironical that this expansion seems to be taking place without proper concern about the use of a resource which should be at the centre of the self-development of the adult. This is at a time when public library resources are most stretched and the advancing but as yet unrealized possibilities of IT for remote access to wide reading, without the need for physical access to libraries, seems to have led to a neglect of present problems and currently realizable opportunities.

CHAPTER 2

Survey of students following postgraduate distance learning courses

Introduction

This chapter presents the findings of a survey of 1,000 DL students, resident throughout the UK and following 21 postgraduate distance courses delivered by 19 UK universities.

The section on use of libraries (p.54) raises some initial issues concerning which libraries are being used and the relationship between library use and course provider expectations. The next section (p.57) takes a broad statistical view of the numeric data, and considers what relationships between variables come to the fore when a large number of possible relationships are examined. The following section (p.60) deals with the textual data arising from the open-ended questions. The final section (p.93) takes one interpretative path through the responses looking at the effect of a variety of factors on the use of libraries. In doing so it draws together some of the findings from the previous sections.

Methodology

In her earlier study of postgraduate DL students, Unwin (1994) had designed a questionnaire in consultation with students, course providers in three universities and university librarians. This questionnaire, which proved to be successful in gathering data from some 350 students, formed the basis of the questionnaire used in this study and was treated as having been a pilot for the much larger survey reported here. Given Unwin's findings about the symbolic importance of library use to DL students, her original questionnaire was extended to seek further quantitative and qualitative data on the range of libraries students use and the problems they encountered in gaining access. In addition, our consultation with course providers and librarians suggested that students may be using libraries beyond the extent which was expected by their course providers and/or in ways which were not properly understood by the other stakeholders.

Design of the questionnaire

The questionnaire was designed by the research team in consultation with librarians and DL students.
  Questions address the following areas:

- characteristics of the respondents, including age, gender, disability and employment;
- course studied and length of study so far;
- expectations regarding library use;
- attitudes towards library use in DL;
- length of journey to nearest libraries in both time and distance;
- actual use of libraries, including number of visits to specified types of library;
- the usefulness of material they contain;
- how students consider themselves to have been received at particular libraries;
- detailed information about the facilities and services they have used;
- training received and wanted;
- access to information technology.

A copy of the questionnaire is included as Appendix 2.

Identification of the sample

The process of identifying the sample of students is worthy of a report in its own right. Ideally, one would have wished to sample systematically the total population of postgraduate DL students, with a proportionate spread of subjects, providing institutions, geographical location of student, age and sex. This might have been possible to achieve if information had been available regarding the characteristics of the total current population. As it is, data regarding DL students are difficult to extract from data on part-time students in general. Figures for DL students are partial and difficult to obtain. Despite the recent growth in DL, statistical returns from universities have not systematically distinguished DL from other part-time students. The Higher Education Funding Council (England) *Profiles of higher education institutions* gives figures for 1992/3, but does not distinguish DL students from other part-timers (HEFCE, 1994).

Indicative figures obtained directly from HEFCE for the year 1992/3 show a total postgraduate DL population for England, excluding the Open University, of 5,228, with 49 universities running such courses. Figures from universities in Scotland show a variable pattern of categorizing distance learning students. The Higher Education Statistical Agency, which deals with university statistical returns across the UK, does not currently allow extraction of national data for DL students.

The OU holds a partial and voluntary database, currently in the process of being updated, of providing institutions, with some information about levels of courses and numbers of students. This database provided the initial points of contact for this study. It is not, however, a statistical database and contains little information about the characteristics of the DL student population. Even as a map of existing courses, it contains some gaps in a rapidly changing field. It does not distinguish courses which are offered entirely overseas, and in some cases does not make clear the level at which courses are offered. For the purposes of our study, a few courses were identified by other means; for example, through advertisements in the press and on the Internet, and by word of mouth.

Another difficulty arose in defining the limits of the study. With increasing flexibility in modes of delivery of university courses there is a growing number of courses, which may not use the term 'distance learning', but whose students experience similar problems of library access. For example, in the field of Education, off-site delivery of Masters degrees and school-based postgraduate initial teacher training are not usually categorized as DL, but their growth and scope need to be recognized.

Some difficulties were encountered in gaining access to students on courses. While follow up letters and phone calls to our initial request elicited a great deal of interest, and willingness to participate in many cases, the additional administrative burden needed to be overcome. One course administrator said:

> Do you realize how many students we have here? I just don't know if we can do it.

After further discussion, this course agreed to distribute the question-naires and to participate in the course provider interviews.

Another large course, which had failed to respond to a number of early enquiries, offered to join the sample at a late stage: the delay had been due simply to pressure of work. A third course, although willing to be involved, had to be excluded because they could only offer a mailing date more than three months away. They had no other admin-istrative machinery available for communicating with students.

In some cases there was difficulty in communicating the relevance of the project. One course provider told us that the study was not relevant to their students since 'they don't need to use libraries'. This course eventually agreed to participate when it was argued that we wanted a representative sample of DL students, and that the informa-tion gained might be of use to them in future planning. They also agreed to participate in our programme of interviews.

Considerable interest in the project has been expressed by the OU, from staff in the library, in the academic departments at Milton Keynes and from several of the regions. The range of opinion within the OU reflects the range across other universities. At one end of the spectrum is the view that materials should be self-contained in order to ensure equality of access for students, while at the other the view is held that independent research in libraries is a core criterion of post-graduate study. Unfortunately, the section of the OU which approves the administration of questionnaires to students by both internal and external researchers concluded that our survey was inappropriate and refused us access to their students.

The sample was finally identified on the basis of willingness to be involved and administrative practicality, although a particular effort was made to pursue courses in as wide a range of disciplines as possible. Out of the 29 different university departments with which we have been in contact, 23 agreed to participate. All of these run courses at Masters level. Two deliver these courses off-site rather than by conventional DL methods.

Distribution of the questionnaires

Initially we requested the names and addresses of students to whom we might send questionnaires. This raised a question of confidentiality in certain cases. We suggested that institutions might mail question-naires to students on our behalf. With most institutions this procedure worked well. With one or two we were left short of information regarding exact numbers distributed to students.

For the courses which agreed to distribute questionnaires on our behalf, as many questionnaires were supplied as the course was believed to have students. This was usually an estimate. In one case questionnaires were supplied for distribution at a particular day school, rather than to be distributed to all enrolled students. In the case of one very large Management course, with numbers of UK resident students estimated at 2,500, we supplied 300 questionnaires to be distributed to the first 300 names generated alphabetically by surname.

An initial batch of questionnaires was distributed in November 1994, with a deadline for returns of December 31st. This was, in retrospect, an ambitious timescale which several institutions found administratively difficult to meet. It was decided to extend the survey to February 1995, and a second batch of questionnaires was distributed after the Christmas break.

In total, approximately 3,000 questionnaires were sent to institutions for distribution to students.

Response rate

Responses were received from students following 21 out of the 23 courses to which questionnaires were sent. We received 1,014 responses in all. Of these, 37 are not currently resident in the UK. This report is therefore based on the responses of 977 students. This is a response rate in excess of 30 per cent, a comparable figure to that achieved in a Canadian survey of DL library use (Burge *et al.*, 1989). This figure conceals widely varying response rates between institutions. Table 1 indicates the variation.

Coding and reliability

Five questions were open-ended. Category systems were derived from extensive reading of the responses and a close reading of a sample of 20. These were tested for reliability within the course team. An initial blind coding exercise on a further sample of 20 questionnaires led to some revisions of the categories.

Table 1: Variation in response rate

University	Course	Response Rate %
F	Dentistry	63.0
N	Education, Adult Education and Speech Science	33.6
M	Management and Computer Science	45.3
E	Construction Management	37.1
J	Management	0.04*

* There are reasons to believe that this exceptionally low figure arises from administrative procedures at this university which resulted in students receiving the questionnaire after the deadline for completion.

Characteristics of the sample

Spread of responses across universities

Table 2 gives a breakdown of number of responses by university rather than by course. The table shows that one institution makes up 30.5 per cent of the sample, while three together make up 55.3 per cent.

Representation of subject areas and length of study

Taking into account the differing response rates between universities surveyed, the sample of respondents reflects the national pattern for a preponderance of students in certain subject areas. The largest group of students was in the area of Management and Business, with Education coming second. The level of returns from Librarianship and Information Science probably reflects the high degree of interest in this project from both course providers and students in this area. Table 3 gives the number of respondents in each subject area and as a percentage of whole group of respondents.

   If the subject areas are grouped, the preponderance of Management and Education is clearer, as shown in Figure 1.

Table 2: Number of responses from universities surveyed

University	Frequency	Per cent of sample
A	2	0.2
B	19	1.9
C	2	0.2
D	5	0.5
E	63	6.4
F	10	1.0
G	4	0.4
H	27	2.8
I	79	8.1
J	29	3.0
K	61	6.2
L	39	4.0
M	86	8.8
N	102	10.4
O	141	14.4
P	300	30.7
Q	8	0.8
Totals:	977	100.0

Questionnaires were distributed to all students registered for study, regardless of how long they had been following their courses. The average number of months of study recorded was 19.5, while half the sample had been studying for 15 months or less.

Table 4 groups months of study into years, showing that the bulk of the respondents had been studying for up to one year, or from 13 months to 2 years (39 per cent and 32.1 per cent respectively). These proportions are roughly halved for year 3, and the numbers for subsequent years are considerably smaller, with the two longest servers being within 7 years of starting.

Geographical spread of students and distance from libraries

Students were asked to record the first digits of their postcode. Students were geographically dispersed throughout the UK, including Northern Ireland, the Isle of Man and the Channel Islands. Only six postal areas (out of 126 indicated by different letter codes) are *not*

Table 3: Number of respondents in each subject area, and percentage of whole group of respondents

Subject Area	Frequency	% of Sample
Careers Guidance	2	0.2
Construction	53	5.4
Arts and Cultural Policy	3	0.3
Dental Radiology	10	1.0
Education (various)	112	11.5
Geographical Information Systems	5	0.5
Law	41	4.2
Library and Information Science	78	8.0
Management	480	49.1
Orthopaedics	8	0.8
Public Relations	27	2.8
Special Educational Needs	136	13.9
Sports Medicine	17	1.7
Speech Science	1	0.1
Total	973	100.0

(Number of respondents for whom subject area was unclear: 4)

represented in this survey: these are Huddersfield, Hull, Kirkwall, Salisbury, Torquay and Shetland.

Distance from host university library
The average distance from the host university library was 141.4 miles. The greatest distance was 400 miles and 7.6 per cent said they lived 300 miles away or more. The most frequently estimated distance was 100 miles. Half of the sample said they lived 105 miles away or less. A substantial minority actually lived quite close to their host library: 17.6 per cent lived 50 miles away or less.

Distance from nearest university library
The majority of students (75 per cent) lived 25 miles or less from their nearest university library, with half of the sample living less than 10 miles away. A small number lived at a great distance: 13 respondents lived 100 miles away or more; one lived 300 miles away.

Figure 1: Grouping of subject areas

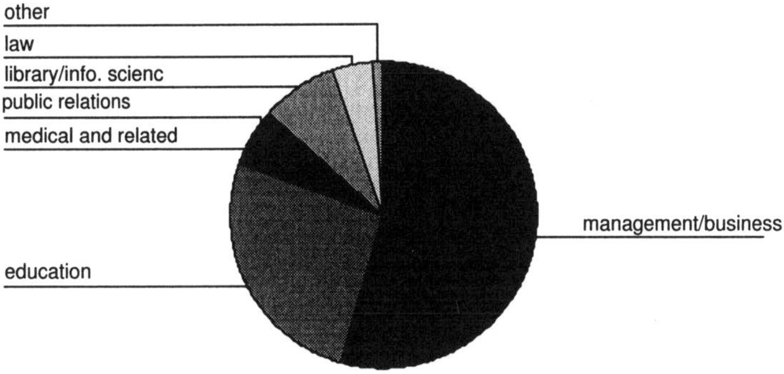

Table 4: Length of study

Period of Study	Frequency	Percent	Cumulative percent
up to 12 months	381	39.0	39.0
year 2 (13 to 24 months)	314	32.1	71.1
year 3	154	15.8	86.9
year 4	74	7.6	94.5
year 5	46	4.7	99.2
year 6	6	0.6	99.8
year 7	2	0.2	100.0
Total	**977**	**100.0**	

Distance from public libraries
The majority (75 per cent) lived 5 miles away or less from a public library. The greatest recorded distance from a public library was 45 miles.

Summary of implications of distance
The data suggest that geographical remoteness from library facilities in general is only an issue for a very small number of students. The geographical accessibility of the public library service is an important

factor. As discussed below, students are making extensive use of this service despite a number of comments about its shortcomings and issues of underfunding. In addition to this, university library facilities are not as geographically remote as the idea of DL might suggest. The vast majority of our sample lived 100 miles away or less from their host university library and 50 miles away or less from their nearest university library.

Why, then is library access such a problem? Although actual distances may not appear great, we also collected information regarding how long particular journeys take, and how realistic students consider it to make such journeys. Factors other than geographical location alone have an important part to play in creating barriers to access to library facilities for DL students. These are discussed later in this chapter.

Age of students

The distribution of age in the sample is of some interest (see Table 5). Approaching half of the sample fell between the ages of 30 and 40. The age range 25 to 45 accounted for more than 75 per cent of the sample. Numbers tailed off slowly after 45 and sharply after 50. These figures suggest that the majority of students were likely to have commitments such as families and jobs which restricted the time available to them for visiting libraries.

Table 5: Distribution of age

Age Group	Frequency	Percent
up to 25	82	8.4
25 to 30	178	18.2
30 to 35	215	22.0
35 to 40	215	22.0
40 to 45	143	14.6
45 to 50	103	10.5
50 to 55	27	2.8
55 to 60	7	0.7
60 to 65	2	0.2
65 and over	5	0.5
Total	977	100.0

Possession of undergraduate degrees and employment situation

A significant minority of students (23.7 per cent) did not have an undergraduate degree. This is worthy of note because such students are unlikely to have had any experience of using a university library and may never have visited a university library before undertaking their present course.

The vast majority (95.9 per cent) were in some kind of paid employment, and most of these worked full time. This reinforces the point made above about other commitments and time available for library use.

Gender distribution

There were slightly fewer women than men: 42 per cent were female.

- *Gender distribution by subject of course.* Sex distribution varied between courses. Table 6 gives a breakdown of gender for Management, Education, Library and Information Science and Other Subjects. While overall 58 per cent of the sample were male, 81.5 per cent of those studying Management were male and only 21.9 per cent of those studying Education were male. There was a preponderance of female respondents in Education and in Librarianship and Information Science, which is out of proportion to the relative numbers of males and females in the overall sample.

Table 6: Crosstabulation of sex by grouped subject areas, with cells showing observed values (in bold) and column percentages

SEX	Total	Manage-ment	Education	Library/Info Science	Other	Row
Male		**433**	**55**	**23**	**51**	**562**
		81.5%	21.9%	29.9%	45.95%	57.9%
Female		**98**	**196**	**54**	**60**	**408**
		18.5%	78.1%	70.1%	54.1%	42.1%
	Column Total	**531**	**251**	**77**	**111**	**970**
		54.7%	25.9%	7.9%	11.4%	100.0%

(Number of missing observations: 7)

This discrepancy is highly statistically significant. (Chi-Square = 285.4; d.f. = 3; p < 0.00001). Any analysis of varying patterns of library use between different subject groups will clearly have to take into account the possibility of differences due to gender.

- *Gender distribution by age.* Figure 2 shows that there was a clearly different shape to the age distributions for male and female students. Numbers of male students seem to peak between 30 and 40, and then collapse in the age group up to 45. Women, by comparison, seem to maintain their involvement in DL over a longer age range. One possible contributory explanation is a difference in male and female career patterns due to family responsibilities. Another is that in Education the possession of a Masters degree may become relevant at a later stage. Any attempt to map disciplinary differences on to library use will have to be carefully considered in the light of gender and age differences.

Figure 2: Gender distribution by age

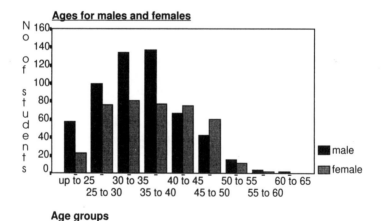

- *Gender distribution by full- and part-time employment.* The vast majority (90.7 per cent) of those in paid employment worked full time. Although there was no significant difference in the numbers of male and female students in paid employment, there was a statistically significant larger number of women in part-time work.

Table 7 shows that, while 43.4 per cent of the sample was female, 86.4 per cent of those in part-time work were female (Chi-square = 67.2; d.f. = 1; p < 0.00001).

Table 7: Crosstabulation of sex by full- or part-time work, with cells showing observed values (in bold) and column percentages

| | | FULL- OR PART-TIME WORK | | |
		full-time	part-time	Row Total
SEX				
Male		**480**	**11**	**491**
		61.0%	13.6%	56.6%
Female		**307**	**70**	**377**
		39.0%	86.4%	43.4%
	Column	**787**	**81**	**868**
	Total	90.7%	9.3%	100.0%

(Number of missing observations: 109)

- *Gender distribution by disability.* Of the sample, 0.9 per cent said that they had a disability which made library access difficult (Table 8).

Table 8: Crosstabulation of sex by disability, with cells showing observed values (in bold) and column percentages

| | | DISABLED | | |
		Yes	no	Row Total
SEX				
Male		**2**	**560**	**562**
		22.2%	58.4%	58.1
Female		**7**	**399**	**406**
		77.8%	41.6%	41.9%
	Column	**9**	**959**	**968**
	Total	0.9%	99.1%	100.0%

(Number of missing observations: 9)

- *Gender distribution by family responsibilities.* Almost half of the sample (46.1 per cent) said that they had domestic responsibilities which made library access difficult. There was no significant difference between the number of males and females in this group.

Use of libraries

Course requirements and student needs: a mismatch of expectations

Interviews with course providers have clearly shown that some believe their students should not need to use libraries because course materials are intended to be entirely self-sufficient. Even where library use is considered commendable, some course providers insist that a course can be successfully completed without using a library.

In our questionnaire we wanted to check how clearly this message came across to students. Figure 3 shows the responses given by students when asked, 'Is it a clearly stated requirement of your course that you make use of libraries?'.

Figure 3: 'Is it a clearly stated requirement of your course that you make use of libraries?'

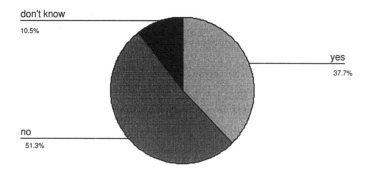

don't know
10.5%

yes
37.7%

no
51.3%

(Missing Cases: 5)

However, Figure 4 shows the answers given when students were asked whether the need was felt to supplement provided course material with additional reading.

Figure 4: Need for additional reading

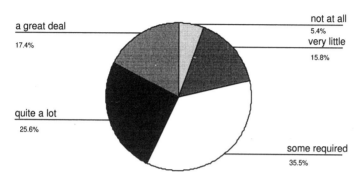

(Missing Cases: 3)

The two charts show a mismatch between what students believe course providers expect, and the extent of the need they actually feel to supplement course material with additional reading. Figure 3 indicates that 37.7 per cent of students said that course providers make clear the need to use libraries. Combined, the 'no' and 'don't know' categories amount to 61.8 per cent of the sample. Asked whether they felt the need to supplement course material with additional reading, 78.5 per cent of the sample said that they needed to do either 'some', 'quite a lot' or 'a great deal'. This mismatch of expectation is illustrated in Table 9.

While the table shows that there is a relationship between course providers' expectations and students' felt need to use libraries, and this relationship is highly statistically significant (Chi Square = 121.86, degrees of freedom = 1^{-1} p < 0.00001), this measure of statistical significance does not indicate the strength of the relationship involved. Examination of the table shows that the majority (67.4 per cent) of students who either feel that the need for additional reading is not made clear, or who are unsure whether it is clear or not, find that they *do* need to do additional reading, at least to some extent. In other words, course provider expectations do *not* predict the need that a large number of students will feel to use libraries. Even where courses do not seem to be expecting students to use libraries, large numbers of students feel the need to use them.

Table 9: Crosstabulation showing need felt to do additional reading against course requirement for library use, with cells showing observed values (in bold) and column percentages

PERCEIVED COURSE REQUIREMENT FOR LIBRARY USE

NEED FELT FOR ADDITIONAL READING		Yes	No/Don't Know	Row Total
Not at all/ Very little		**10** 2.7%	**196** 32.6%	**206** 21.3%
Some/Quite at lot/ A great deal		**358** 97.3%	**405** 67.4%	**763** 78.7%
	Column Total	**368** 38.0%	**601** 62.0%	**969** 100.0%

(Number of missing observations: 8)

Extent of reported use and variation in use between libraries

The majority (72.5 per cent) said that they had already used library facilities for their course. Of those who said that they had not used a library so far, 61.5 per cent said that they expected to do so in the future. In all, 904 students said that either a library had already been used for the course, or that one would be used in the future. This represents 93 per cent of the sample. Figure 5 shows the number of reported visits made in the last three months. The number who had used a library at least once in the last three months is rather smaller than those who had used a library at some time for the course, but still represents nearly two-thirds of the sample.

Table 10: Total number of visits to different types of library

Host University	494
Nearest University	1,026
Public Libraries	1,538
Specialist Libraries	1,066

Table 10 shows that the host library was the least used, with extensive use being made of nearest universities and specialist libraries. Public libraries are used for DL courses more frequently than any other kind.

Figure 5: Reported visits to libraries in the last three months

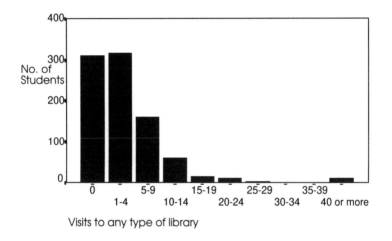

Visits to any type of library

Sifting the numeric data for statistically significant relationships

Crosstabulating the data

The analysis shows that there is a large number of highly statistically significant small degrees of relationship between variables. This finding indicates both the complexity of the field and the interrelatedness of several of the measures. The strongest relationships, with probability values for Chi Square smaller than 0.00001 and a measure of degree of correlation (Phi or Cramer's V) in excess of 0.24, are discussed below.

- *Subject and sex.* It was noted early in the study that students on Management courses were more likely to be male, while students studying Education and Librarianship were more likely to be female. The strength of this relationship, in comparison to the others observed, has implications for the interpretation of the data in general.

- *Subject and having received training as part of the course.* This is probably particularly affected by the number of Library and Information Science students, whose course is necessarily concerned with the use of libraries. Further analysis of this relationship would be useful.

- *Students' felt need to supplement course material and whether a library has been used.* The strength of this relationship is a matter of no surprise, since the questions are related. It is, however, a reassuring indication of the validity of the data.

- *Visits to a public library and perception of usefulness of material it contains.* It is of some interest that this shows a stronger degree of relationship than for other types of library. It fits with the observation that usefulness of material is most salient in relation to public libraries: some students make strong judgements about the lack of relevant material in public libraries, while others find a good deal of value in the public library resources that are available to them.

- *Estimated distance from host library and practicality of journey.* This is another example of related measures showing an unsurprisingly high degree of relationship. It is worth noting, however, that for journeys to other libraries, the observed relationships were not as strong, suggesting that other issues come into play when students make such judgements. This is explored further later in the chapter.

- *Other variables related to subject.* In addition to sex and having received training as part of the course, subject is related to a number of other measures, including course provider expectations, the need felt to use libraries, and a measure of number of visits. In addition, it is related to access to information technology. Students in certain subject areas are more likely to have access to a networked PC at home and at work.

- *Other variables related to training.* As well as its relationship with subject, students who have received training are more likely to have a copy of the host library's information pack, and are more likely to expect their courses to require use of libraries and reading beyond the course material.

- *Variables related to attitudes.* Subject of course is related to whether or not students expect the course to include all the necessary reading material. Also, students who feel the need to supplement course material are more likely to want access to a university 'like other HE students'.

- *Variables related to number of library visits.* This measure of library use is discussed in more detail later in this chapter. Students who have visited the host library are more likely to believe it contains useful material. A similar relationship exists for specialist libraries and for the nearest university library. In addition, students who feel a stronger need to supplement the course material are more likely to have visited the nearest university library. This strength of relationship does *not* exist for the host library. Students who find material useful at their nearest university library are also more likely to have visited a specialist library.

Multivariate analysis

The calculations presented and discussed above are only concerned with relationships between two variables at a time. While there appears to be a relationship between, for example, sex and whether a library has been used, it is possible that this relationship disappears when crosstabulations within subject areas are examined. A number of crosstabulations within different levels of the same variable should be examined before too many conclusions are drawn.

Looking, for example, at how sex, age and subject area interact in relation to a particular outcome variable is a still more complex matter. In order to examine the influences on extent of use of particular types of libraries and on access to information technology of a number of potential explanatory variables, an analysis was commissioned from Sheffield University Statistical Services Unit. The results of this are presented in Appendix 1.

The analysis suggests that neither sex nor age are determinants of library use. The analysis also casts doubt on the idea of subject as an explanatory factor. Visits to all types of library appear to be influenced by the student's felt need to supplement the course material. Course provider expectation is a factor for all except the host library. Geographical distance is an additional factor for both nearest and host university libraries. Visits to the host university library are also related to length of time of study and whether or not training has been received.

Access to computers and networked computers seems to be clearly subject-related, with access to any computer either at home or at work being more likely for those following courses in Management, and Library and Information Science. As might be expected, the latter are more likely to have access to a networked computer. Additionally, overall, male students are more likely to have access to networked computers.

Issues arising from the open-ended questions

How students felt they were treated at libraries: 'No special arrangements'

Respondents were asked to say how they had been received at each of the types of library they had used. This question generated a much wider range of responses than we had expected. Students did not restrict themselves to immediately relevant responses, but used the space provided to raise a wide range of issues. The responses therefore need to be considered in relation to the material which appears in the section below on 'Additional comments'.

The wide range of responses presents problems for a thorough summary of the material. Discussion in the course team generated a list of 22 topic codes, along with an 'other' category and a category for non-response. These are listed in Table 11 with the percentages of the sample (including non-responses) to which each code category was assigned. (Column totals equal more than 100 per cent because some comments were assigned more than one code.)

A substantial minority of students made generalized positive comments about the manner in which they had been received. However, a relatively large number of respondents indicated that they had not been treated 'as a DL student' at all. Responses in this category varied from very negative remarks about the absence of special arrangements which should be expected, to comments which indicate that the student would neither wish nor expect such special treatment, such as 'no different from any other user' and 'just like a normal student'.

A relatively large number of respondents indicated that their public library is inadequately resourced for their needs: 89 in comparison to the 6, 13 and 11 who made such comments about host, nearest university and specialist libraries. Similarly, 33 made negative comments about using the public libraries for interlibrary loan compared to very small numbers making such comments in relation to other libraries.

Training

Nearly one third (308) made some comment about training already received. For some students, library training was not seen to be necessary:

> Don't feel this should be necessary—I was taught to use a library at primary school.

> Only an idiot would not be able to use a library.

> I don't think it should constitute part of the course.

A number of comments referred to training received as part of a previous course, most typically as undergraduates:

> I have just completed a degree at xxxx. Training was given for the course.

For a small section of the sample, professional background was relevant:

> As a professional librarian of 20 years, not really necessary.

However, even librarians might not be as well prepared as is commonly supposed:

> It is assumed that we know, but I don't because my main work is in a school library which is not automated.

Table 11: Response Codes for Treatment as a Distance Learning Student

	Host	Nearest	Public	Other
1. Non-specific or unclassified positive comment, Anything from 'fine', 'satisfactory' and 'okay' to 'excellent'. Includes comments about the attitude of staff, as well as the nature of services or procedures	26.7%	13.6%	22.6%	16.1%
2. Non-specific or unclassified negative comment, anything from 'indifferent' to 'second class' and 'rude'	8.7%	0.8%	33.8%	6.9%
3. Special DL collection or exhibition, e.g. Organized for residential	0.3%	0%	0%	0%
4. Special DL loan periods	0.4%	0%	0%	0%
5. Telephone service which assists remote access which may or may not be set up specifically for DL students	0.7%	0.1%	0%	0%
6. Postal service, either routinely offered or offered in a special case	0.9%	0.2%	0.1%	0.1%
7. Absence of a special DL arrangement or treatment, including lack of special treatment, regardless of whether this is intended as criticism e.g. 'no different from any other user', 'just like a normal student' and 'no concession to distance learners'	8.9%	1.5%	55.3%	3.1%
8. Positive comment about opening hours	0%	0.2%	0%	0%
9. Negative comment about opening, including evening closure and closure during weekend school	0.8%	0.1%	0%	0.3%
10. Problems gaining any access, even for reference only	0.5%	0.2%	0%	1.6%
11. Library can be used for reference only, because borrowing is not allowed or severely restricted	0.3%	0.6%	0%	7.6%
12. No/limited database access	0%	0%	0%	0.3%
13. No/limited access to interlibrary loan	0%	0%	0.1%	0.1%
14. Negative comment about interlibrary loan service, slow, books don't arrive, too expensive, staff not happy about doing it	0%	0.1%	3.4%	0.1%
15. Positive comment about interlibrary loan, including cheapness, speed	0%	0.7%	1.5%	0%
16. Informal arrangement or special arrangement for a particular group including local teachers	0%	0.1%	0%	0.4%
17. Arrangement through another person who has membership, friend or spouse	0%	0.1%	0%	1.0%
18. Library is at place of work, librarian, lecturer or other professional with workplace library	0.1%	2.3%	0.4%	3.0%
19. Positive comment about stock	0.4%	0.6%	0.6%	0.2%
20. Negative comment about stock and specialist subject knowledge of librarian	0.6%	1.3%	9.1%	1.1%
21. High cost, including membership and returning by post	0.4%	0.5%	0.3%	1.9%

22. Low cost	0%	0%	0.1%	0%
23. Other comment about library use	0.6%	0.5%	0.7%	0.5%
24. No comments, or comments which indicate that the library has not been used such as 'N/A' or 'not used'	58.3%	80.5%	61.2%	63.2%

A few expanded on the absence or inadequacy of training. Comments suggest that training is *ad hoc*, there is no minimum standard and it ranges from 'Very poor and insulting' to 'Structured day with head librarian and staff'. For some, the timing of training given was an issue:

> Training in use of host library (after 1 year of course)

> Librarian demonstrated computer facilities and interactive video/CD-ROM. Now forgotten.

> No, but an opportunity was provided on one of the residential weekends in xxxx. I missed it because of its timing—Friday afternoon.

Just over one quarter (260 students) amplified their responses about training they would like to have received at the beginning of their courses. Responses varied in their degree of specificity, but covered a relatively restricted range of issues. Treatment of the issues frequently went beyond the intent of the question to make requests for the setting up of services or arrangements which do not currently exist for all or most students. The responses were coded according to categories in Table 12, with a minimum of one and a maximum of three codes assigned per comment.

A minority (11.8 per cent) of students made comments which amounted to requests for services or information with special relevance for DL students, including reciprocal arrangements and host library services for the remote user.

A similar size group (9 per cent) made comments referring to the kind of library services to which a full-time resident student might have access, such as: 'the library catalogue system'; 'subject librarian'; 'how to get books initially on loan'; and 'a clear explanation of how journals are catalogued and stored in the university library'.

We were surprised at the number of students (a further 9 per cent) requesting the most basic information about library provision and services. For example:

Table 12: Response Codes for Library Guidance Question

	Number	Percent
1. Would like to have been told that the library and/or extensive reading would be essential/desirable (including comments about the unexpected nature of the need for use of a library)	6	0.6
2. A request for general information of any kind about what a library can offer or how to use it, suggesting a very low level of awareness of how a library might be used to support study, or indicating that virtually no information of any kind has been given	84	9.0
3. A request for specific information about the usual library stock or services (e.g. journals, theses, databases, CD-ROM, literature searching)	88	9.0
4. Information about networked services or remote electronic access/ JANET	31	3.2
5. Information about host library special DL arrangements/ services such as postal services, including requests to set up such services, as well as information about existing services	29	3.0
6. Information about reciprocal arrangements, or how to get access to another university library	55	5.6
7. More/earlier/some training	5	0.5
8. Other	5	0.5

As a mature student re-entering academic system I felt intimidated and unsure how to access library facilities and their full potential. I would have welcomed some *discreet* teaching in this area.

At the beginning of the course we didn't know what we needed guidance on.

I would like to have known that no library usage was organized.

Not so much specific, but general basics, like how to use the online catalogue (I've just about got it), how to find things like journal articles and how to use a CD-ROM (I haven't a clue where to start.)

An outline of what services the host library provides would have been useful for orienting myself.

The usage of standard facilities in public libraries.

A detailed explanation of the facilities available from a modern library.

Such comments seem to suggest for some students the need for general orientation regarding what a library can offer.

Charges for library services

From the closed questions we know that 196 respondents felt that they had been put off using library services by charges. Students were also asked to give details of any charges that had put them off using library services. Responses are presented in Table 13.

Table 13: Codes and frequencies for details of off-putting library charges

	Frequency	Percent
Cost of membership/reader's ticket	31	3.2
Cost of borrowing	16	1.6
Cost of database search/printout	10	1.0
Cost of ILL	20	2.0
Cost of photocopying	13	1.4
Fines	4	0.4
Other negative comments about costs	78	8.0
Complaint about a particular library	15	1.5
Other comments: happy about costs	16	1.5
No comments	794	81.3
Total	**977**	**100.0**

The large 'other negative comment about costs' category shows the difficulty we found in categorizing these comments. The largest single category after this is the cost of membership. If this is combined with borrowing costs, 23.2 per cent of the comment codes assigned (excluding no comment) concern the costs of membership rights. The next largest category after this is the cost of interlibrary loan.

Additional comments

Over one third of respondents (377) made comments under this heading. Comments were coded using the categories in Table 14. Each comment was given at least one code, with a maximum upper limit being set only by the number of codes available. Thus single responses were frequently multiple-coded, if the comment seemed to relate to more than one issue.

The four most frequently mentioned issues are indicated in the table in bold. The largest three groups of comments are discussed first below, while the fourth, relating to time issues, is discussed last in this section.

Reciprocal arrangements

The overwhelming concern of our respondents was with access to nearby university libraries or specialist libraries. This concern seemed to outweigh any concern to see services at their host library developed. The following comments, selected from those put forward by 103 students, refer to reciprocal arrangements with other university libraries. Several of these indicate that it should be the responsibility of the host university to make such arrangements.

> Access to the local university who do have relevant books would have been very helpful.

> Linking with other libraries should be more readily available—not piecemeal.

> I believe that course directors should do more with their colleagues in other institutions to open up library services to DL students so students can access a local service without having to make personal arrangements.

> It would have been useful if registration on the DL course gave one unlimited access to local university libraries.

> Reciprocal arrangements between universities with DL students seems only common sense.

Table 14: Codes and frequencies for additional comments

Code Description	Codes No	Codes %	Comments %
All necessary *reading is or should be included* in course material and/or set books	33	4.3	8.8
Access to a *library is or should be needed.* Materials cannot or should not be completely inclusive. Using library is enjoyable or valuable	63	8.3	16.7
Surprised to find library needed. Shocked, might have reconsidered if difficulty known	7	0.9	1.9
Comment about *dissertation* or project	25	3.3	6.6
Comment about *access to nearby university* library, including requests for information or reciprocal arrangements	103	13.5	27.3
Comment about *special access to library facilities*, including specialist or professional library, workplace library and access to a university library because of special status including ex-student and personal or professional connection	68	8.9	18.0
Comment about *public library*	25	3.3	6.6
Comment about *need for information*, including membership of host, general and specific information or training. (Excluding information about reciprocal arrangements)	38	5.0	10.1
Comment about *distance*, including geographical/regional isolation, and journey time	43	5.7	11.4
Lack of time* due to work, family commitments, or pressure of course and included reading itself	55	7.2	14.6
Comment about time taken for *interlibrary loan*	10	1.3	2.7
Comment about *time taken to get/find necessary reading* without or in addition to specific mention of speed of interlibrary loan	21	2.8	5.6
Problem of short *loan periods* or need for longer ones, including cost of fines	13	1.7	3.5
Library closed, longer *opening hours* needed or outside usual working hours	25	3.3	6.6
Comment about *course or library fees*, either happy or willing to pay, or unhappy about cost	32	4.2	8.5
Comment about *buying books*, whether positive or negative about cost	42	5.5	11.1
Other comment about money, except fines	9	1.2	2.3
Comment about *residential or day school*	17	2.2	4.5
Comment about *telephone service*	4	0.5	1.1
Comment about *postal service*, or need for such a service	20	2.6	5.3
Comment about use of *CD-ROM*	8	1.1	2.1
Comment about *Internet, Janet, dial-in*, virtual library	31	4.1	8.2
Emphatic *positive comment* about a particular course, library or service	23	3.0	6.1
Other issues	46	6.0	12.2
Total Codes Assigned	**761**		

. . . it should be the responsibility of the host university to ensure that all its students should have equal access to university standard libraries.

I think other universities should allow us to use their libraries when doing a DL course. Universities should have a joint arrangement whereby DL students can utilize the facilities of any UK universities, including borrowing books.

I have this naive view that education and their library services should be open to all.

It would be useful to have some arrangement with the nearest university library which would allow full use of their facilities . . . without extra subscription.

If a person is in HE in any capacity I believe they should have free access to all the HE library facilities, and I believe that there should be reciprocity between all HE libraries. I feel strongly that this is a fundamental right, and that any compromise is a dangerous policy.

Would it not be to everyone's advantage for universities, certainly those offering part-time, modular or DL courses, to set up some sort of reciprocal networking of facilities, resources and access?

Membership should be made available across the university library networks for students on DL courses.

With the increase in DL courses, it is time for reciprocal facilities to be made available.

. . . it would be useful if as university students (part-time, full-time, DL, etc.) we could have some form of library ticket that is transferable/can be used at any academic institution.

The following comments refer to the limited range of services to which external users sometimes have access.

I have requested and been allowed use of a local university library for reading but not for borrowing—of no real use.

I felt very frustrated that I couldn't use the full library services at local universities when facilities were there.

I just go in and use (the library) as a reading/photocopying facility. This is very limiting, i.e. I cannot borrow, despite being willing to pay.

I only got limited access to the local university library on strength of previous contacts so I felt I could not probe further or push for greater access.

I was appalled by my treatment by the university. They wanted a lot of money for second class access to the library.

Universities do not seem keen to let students of other universities use their libraries.

Some students are put off by the manner in which they are received, for example:

I have approached the university to see if I could get access to their library but was put off by the person I spoke to. Although friendly and sympathetic she said it was unlikely that I would be allowed to use the university library. I was so discouraged I did not take the matter further.

When telephoning other academic libraries I have occasionally felt as though the distance learner is considered as a less than serious student.

Special connections

In gaining access to libraries, 68 commented on how they made use of special connections as a means of getting access to library facilities, of which 41 were work-related connections. The sample included a number of librarians, many of whom would be at a considerable advantage.

> I am a librarian of a hospital and employed by a university library service, therefore questions of access and training don't really apply!

> Fortunately, I run a library so I do not need the host university library.

However, not all librarians were so well placed:

> As a practising librarian as well as a student, I appreciate the problems involved. For my own course, with a dissertation containing a substantial review, it has been difficult to access material and without the assistance of [a specialist library] I could not have continued—my own library's stock and ILL budget could not cope!

Other professional groups commented on workplace libraries or professional libraries.

> Without our service library the course would have been impossible.

> I may be unusual in that for the first year of the two year course I was employed with employer sponsoring courses and with good in-house relevant research material.

> It might help you to know that I currently work at another university. This makes my situation different to that of most DL students.

> I am privileged in that as an employee of xxxx I have access to the medical library in xxxx.

> I was/am fortunate in having access to our own library in the careers service.

> Since I work in an FE college I can access interlibrary loan and photocopies of journal articles etc., so, if I can allow time, I don't have a problem.

> My company has a library function which obtains books and copies of articles from the British Library for me.

> The ability to use a works-based library has been a tremendous advantage . . . without this the answers would change in the questionnaire.

A feature of these responses is the frequency with which such access is described as fortunate or untypical.

Some used ex-student status as a means of gaining access, for example:

> As a graduate of my local university I have access to its library and facilities should I require them, which means I probably don't face the problems some DL students do.

> Even my previous university . . . of which I am an alumni (and I pay an annual fee for this) has restricted use of the library for former students and alumni.

Other students have used personal connections, for example:

> My husband has access at work to xxxx University library.

> I have had no problems gaining access to a library due to my partner. I have no idea how difficult it would have been otherwise.

> I had to rely on a friend to gain access to the library.

> I have relied upon a friend accessing books/articles for me from a university (40 miles away) where she works. Without this I would have had great difficulty.

Extent of need for libraries

A significant number of students (63) reiterated or emphasized the point that library use is necessary or valued. Where the question of the inclusiveness of course materials was referred to, this tended to be presented in a negative light with the suggestion that access to libraries for wider reading would be preferred. Some referred to the pleasure or challenge of library use. Others ranged from those indicating that it is either impractical or undesirable to expect supplied course material to be all inclusive, to those who commented on the disappointing quality of their own work which they felt was due to library access problems.

The following comments underline the inherent value of library use.

> Part of the enjoyment of doing a DL course is using any appropriate source of reference you can find.

> I have used libraries for personal development and only referred to material relating to the course just out of interest in knowing more about different terminology, etc., used outside those in the university's reading materials, thereby widening my horizons.

> Access to an academic library with space to work and research in would be wonderful.

Some comments referred to the impossibility of completing a course solely from the materials supplied.

> It is impossible, in my opinion, to satisfactorily complete an M.Ed. course without access to relevant books, journal articles. As a DL student, much better facilities are urgently required.

> 'A DL course should include . . .' Impossible. It is essential to be able to search out your own references (and develop the ability to do so).

I do not believe that a typical degree course is likely to be satisfactorily completed without at least some supplementary library material.

. . . to participate in this course of study access to a wide range of material (of my own choosing) is vital.

. . . I find that at times I need to read a different text either as a way of seeking clarification on certain topics, or getting things, or getting a simplified version of things . . .

I feel that the supplied material for my course covers the appropriate ground, but I like to clarify points and obtain an alternative view by using other material.

While the course material provided contained all the required reading, I feel it is important to supplement these through further reading, especially in area of special interest or to clear up uncertainties in the course material.

I am finding elements . . . quite difficult and would like access to further reference materials to clarify issues.

Whilst DL course materials include most of the information required for the course, the absence of discussion of the course can mean gaps need to be filled. A wider reading access will help.

. . . any course is only a beginning point, therefore access to a range of background information is essential, especially in an informal browsing manner.

Some students suggested that the quality of their own work would be likely to suffer from lack of library access:

At the end of my course now. My work has disappointed me—poor quality—much to do with both lack of time but also lack of good access to decent resources.

Those of us who live at a great distance from the host university and in a rural area are greatly disadvantaged . . .

journals are just not available and therefore assignments are marked down because reading has not been wide enough.

Good library facilities can make the difference between being confident in approaching coursework and supplementing arguments with reference to literature, and scraping through.

I worked in Saudi Arabia for two years and the great problem was to find anything resembling a library. I was feeling slightly persecuted when a marker commented on two essays from Saudi that they lacked further reading. AAARGH!

Other students suggested that they would consider the inclusion of all necessary course material as highly undesirable:

. . . I would not expect all the necessary books, publications and so on to be supplied. That would severely limit the scope of my study . . .

I think it would be narrow minded to expect all the course material to provide everything needed.

My course is very self-contained and one can pass exams without reading widely. However at times it concerns me that this is possible, particularly at masters level. My use of libraries will be to further my knowledge in areas of specific interest, rather than to meet the requirements of the course.

Theoretically it should be better to familiarize oneself with other writings in the field, but the course is only marked on adherence to, and regurgitation of, the course materials so in academic terms other reading is pointless unless it agrees with the course material.

Self contained courses

A minority of students (33) said that their courses either were or should be self-contained, with course material and texts supplying all the necessary material. For example:

> Distance learning courses should provide all the necessary reading materials for the benefit of those of us studying in rural areas who cannot access library facilities easily.

> . . . reading material should be provided, I have no time to look for it.

> As a DL student, I would expect the course fee to include all relevant materials, notes, etc. to allow a well prepared student to pass the examinations without recourse to additional material.

Positive comments

Although 24 students made emphatically positive comments about their courses or the library services they had made use of, almost all of these comments are prefaced by complaints, or lie in the shadow of negative considerations. They were often quickly followed by a 'but' or 'however', as the following examples indicate:

> My host university course is the best I have seen but it is hard work due to the problems with library access.

> The course I am following is well structured with guidance on required reading (we still have to get hold of it ourselves). Academic libraries have failed to resolve the difficulties . . .

> My local library has been very helpful. When telephoning other academic libraries I have occasionally felt as though the distance learner is considered as a less than serious student.

The dissertation

Twenty-five comments referred to the particular need for library support when approaching a dissertation or project. The following comment points to a contradiction in the marketing of some DL courses:

> Most DL courses are marketed as being suitable for 'busy executives' which is fine if the course is highly structured and photocopied 'readings' are provided—but requirements for open-ended dissertations are not compatible with this mode of study. These courses should include more library support—and research methodology training—if theses and dissertations are required.

Some had clearly been taken by surprise at the difficulties surrounding library access:

> I didn't expect it to be so difficult.

> I would like to have been made aware that I would require some library facilities for research.

> I had underestimated how difficult it would be for me to use a library . . .

> I was very disappointed with the service I received . . .

> I would think very seriously before doing another DL course due to the difficulty of actually borrowing books from local university libraries.

> In the future I would not enrol for a DL course unless there was better provision for support materials.

Public libraries

Twenty-five comments referred to public libraries. Of these, nine made broadly positive comments, while 13 were broadly negative:

Thus far in my course, most of my requirements have been met by course materials provided and the public library.

The public library is not specialized enough.

Sadly, I feel that the level of services provided by public libraries has declined in the last 20 years and is symptomatic of the level of importance our present government attributes to education and particularly self-education. My local public library *should* be able to support more sophisticated needs than fiction, video and record lending, particularly with regard to modern business and engineering publications and statistical references.

Why can't my local library have a computer link with all universities on a network for information gathering?

Even ordering specialist books has proved difficult—I have ordered from county libraries and out of county but everything takes an inordinate amount of time.

Distance

For some students (43) the difficulties presented by distance or geographical isolation were worthy of note. For example:

Living on the Isle of Man provides real difficulties for those wishing to take part in DL courses.

I live in a rural area and small town libraries do not cater adequately for specialist subjects.

Distance learning is difficult in Cumbria because of the lack of a local university . . .

I live in Jersey, which makes anything other than postal borrowing or electronic data transfer impossible.

The reason for studying this course is that there is no similar course available in Ireland.

> As an engineer in my present role I am required to work
> extensively overseas away from my normal site . . .

> The nearest medical school library is 125 miles away.

Residential periods

The inclusion of residential or day schools in a course can provide an
important opportunity for students to use their host university library,
as these comments indicate:

> I have very rarely used the host library except during
> summer schools.

> I feel that there should be time set aside, on one of the first
> residentials, for describing the library service to those who
> may not be so familiar with the service.

> Having been offered access to the host university library
> on the final residential was useful but frustrating. It would
> have been more useful if access were timetabled into all
> residential weekends.

There are, however, limitations of library access during these
periods to be considered:

> My DL course has involved short residential elements—
> often the library has not been available, e.g. because they
> have overlapped with university student terms.

> We have a study weekend once a year and I would have
> liked to have used the . . . library, but it is closed at week-
> ends!

> The university library was never open at the weekend
> when the study sessions were held.

Telephone and postal services

The use of telephone and postal services for accessing the host university library was referred to by 24 students. In the few cases where

telephone services were specifically mentioned (three) these referred to either poor or absent services.

> . . . the host library was unbelievably unhelpful over the telephone—couldn't even tell me if a book was in stock so I could drive up and get it.

> Telephone skills could perhaps be improved!

> As a DL student juggling with a number of things, I would have benefited from, for example, contacting the library by phone so that articles, etc. could be sent to me at a minimum cost.

Eleven students made a direct request for a postal service. For example:

> I feel it is the duty of the host university to provide at least a postal service to their students.

> Distance learning students should be able to *either* borrow and return books by post free of charge or the price of a 25p stamp.

> I think a monthly or quarterly reading list with copies available by post is what is lacking.

> I would like a full postal service with my host university library—I would be willing to pay for postage.

Information and training

Students clearly need more support in order to use libraries effectively, as the following comments indicate:

> I would welcome information on holiday closures, etc. as part of course mail.

> I am not really aware of my entitlements in relation to the host university library.

Students should be introduced to the librarian responsible for DL and full details of service possible given personally.

I would like advice on alternatives, e.g. can I use a local university library?

A library information pack would be of tremendous value.

I was not aware that [students on my course] are entitled to full student loan privileges at the [host] Library.

I still don't have a library card. We should be sent one as a standard practice, not as a special request.

When starting to learn a new subject I don't know what is available or where to start looking.

The library has been poorly marketed to students on the course.

One student offered this solution:

. . . might I suggest some thought is given to including a module early in the course whereby instructions and practical tasks are set that would for the rest of the course set the student up with sufficient knowledge and confidence that the maximum value would be obtained from the available reference facilities for the rest of the course. Such a module would be most useful in *external* courses.

Information technology

Any training in library skills also needs to include training in IT, as the following comment indicates:

The little time I did spend in the host university library indicated the wide range of information on computer databases. I was hitherto computer illiterate but found it fascinating and intend to use such databases in future to further my own personal learning.

Only two comments referred to currently successful experience in using online facilities, while the remaining 32 references to Internet or JANET access were either requests for information or littered with 'shoulds', 'woulds' and 'maybes':

> . . . would be very interested in online catalogue, JANET and training for JANET. All three are theoretically available but I have no access point currently.

> Perhaps computerization may be a future answer.

> The ideal would be electronic access to all materials in the university library!

> Linking home computer to JANET, etc. was not offered as an option—nor was it explained that we might be able to access JANET from office computers.

> If I had my own PC, I would consider access to JANET.

> Access to a library via a PC would be extremely useful and worth paying a fairly considerable amount to obtain.

> Distance learning students should be pioneers in the use (and so in shaping) the 'virtual library'.

> The price should include hardware, software, installation and configuration time, running phone line to PC, telephone call consumption, Internet subscription, wasted consumables during learning curve, any additional database interrogation fees and time spent mining such databases for hoped for 'golden nuggets'.

> Inexpensive online search facilities and ability to download papers/articles via home computer would be the ultimate solution for DL.

> The challenge is going to be affordable access to these online services.

I feel that my DL has been aided considerably by having access to library at work and being able to browse from my computer at work. I was also able to buy a computer when I started studying. Both these factors have given me an enormous advantage and I have been very aware that for many other people these facilities are not available—shows up lots of equal opportunities issues.

Financial cost

Students are divided in terms of their attitudes to buying extra reading for their courses. Comments ranged from the wholly negative to those that were positive about the value of personal ownership of texts. Between these extremes, responses were qualified in various ways. For example, some thought that it was desirable to buy certain texts, but that the need for library access remained for wider reading, including use of journals. Others were keen to buy books that might be used as constant sources of reference, but wanted to be sure that they were making the right choices and might need library access for browsing purposes. The crucial role of libraries in supplying access to out of print books was also mentioned. The following comments reflect the range of attitudes:

> Out of desperation I have bought quite a number of books for my course and also subscribed to additional journals—this is not easy for me financially but I have felt it to be the only option to gain certain access and quick access to needed resources.

> The course I am currently doing was advertised as an 'all inclusive price'. However, as I am self-financing, it was a shock to find out after I commenced the course that a further seven books totalling approximately £300 were required, plus additional reading (mainly specialist texts) which either have to be purchased or reserved at a price (nominal).

> I have had to purchase around £200 of books for the two-year course and do not mind this, but this information needs to be supplemented by current materials which is what libraries should present.

I buy books at the moment as getting them is difficult but need to know booklist for units in advance and it is personally costly. Also you do not know how much you will need them.

If I use a library it tends to be to get journal articles, get away from the noise at home, use books, but buy them if they prove very useful.

I prefer to buy books to avoid renewal but this is only practical if it is going to be a constant source of reference.

I am in the fortunate position of being in mature, full-time employment. I buy the books I need. I will probably only use the library when books required are out of print (as some are).

I have managed to get the Technical Library of our company to purchase for me all the books on the recommended reading list (to date) which have in effect become my personal copies for the duration of my course.

I've spent more on new books, but I have them all the time without other people's annotations!

I may be unusual in that for the first year of a two year course I was employed with employer sponsoring courses and with good in-house salary. The high cost of the basic course residentials perhaps places the course out of reach of low paid or unemployed but should they undertake such a course any additional costs, however marginal, may affect their ability to adequately access research material or general reading.

Several students (31) referred to the question of fees, either for the course or for additional library services, and 25 of these made negative comments about the effect of additional charges. For example:

I hope the underlying reason for this survey is not to judge what prices students are willing to pay for facilities and set them accordingly.

I desperately hope that the point of this questionnaire is not to charge for library services.

There are many additional costs to DL and the use of libraries should be included in the course fees.

Long DL is becoming a very competitive market and introducing separate library charges for xxxx's course will not make commercial sense.

I do use a local university library as an external student (no fee this year but £70 next year) and I feel that this fee should be part of the course fee, i.e. an agreement between HE institutions for distance learners.

I don't know why the university libraries can't establish commonality and for me to transfer my library fee or a part of it to my nearest university library. I object to paying twice over and paying fees for a library I can't use.

A small number of students did, however, suggest that paying extra fees might be helpful:

I don't mind paying a bit extra on course fees for speed and accessibility of information.

. . . it should be fairly straightforward to set up a library support network so that all students had borrowing facilities at their nearest university . . . a small extra fee or inclusion in course fees to provide this shouldn't be too much to arrange.

A further nine references were made to money matters, including: general complaints about lack of money; the cost of travel; the cost of literature searching; underfunding of public libraries; the relationship between cost and convenience of a course; the cost of fines; and a plea for a system of getting hold of second-hand books from former students.

Time

After reciprocal arrangements, time was the issue raised most emphatically and with the greatest frequency. Apart from travelling times to libraries, our questionnaire did not ask questions about time constraints under which students work. In the words of one student:

> This questionnaire doesn't relate at all to 'time' available while doing a DL course.

The coding scheme differentiated between a variety of time issues. We coded separately comments about opening times of libraries, comments about loan periods, comments about time taken for interlibrary loans, other comments about time taken to get hold of recommended reading, and other comments about time constraints which were further analyzed according to the scheme described below.

Opening times of libraries
The 25 comments which referred to opening times of libraries were almost entirely complaints about restricted opening, the difficulty of fitting this in with a work routine, closure during residential schools and restricted opening during vacations. For example:

> The local university library is only open 08.45–17.00 hours—my working hours—and I have to take holiday leave in order to visit it.

> The hours of opening are the main problem. For myself, with a full-time job, it can be difficult to visit the library during the week. Weekend opening at some time at all university libraries would be desirable.

> Distance learning, being a 12 month/year activity, can be problematic during vacation periods when university libraries have restricted opening hour and borrowing services.

Borrowing periods
These comments included requests for extended loan periods bearing in mind the situation of the DL student, as well as complaints that

short loan collections were effectively unborrowable for the student who cannot make frequent visits. For example:

> The library operates a 7 day loan facility on popular books which sometimes means I cannot use the book as I cannot return it within the time limit and fines are expensive.

> . . . many of the titles required for the course are in the DL short loan collection. This means that any books I borrow on Saturday need to be returned on Monday—which in fact means they are 'unborrowable'.

Interlibrary loans
Comments here relate to public, university and workplace libraries. For example:

> Even ordering books has proved difficult—I have ordered from county libraries and out of county but everything takes an inordinate amount of time.

> Trying to do an in-depth postgraduate study such as a dissertation is initially impossible when you have to wait four or five months for a book through interlibrary loan.

> When I started I thought that I could get by with using my local library network for extra reading materials. This has proved rather impractical due to delays in receiving ordered loan materials.

Pursuing reading matter
Some comments referred to time factors in getting reading material, other than those related to interlibrary loan. The time it takes to reserve books generally is an issue. For example:

> Ordering books takes too long and is too restrictive.

> I didn't realize how long it would take books that I reserved to be made available to me—some arrived after assignments that they were needed for had been handed in.

> Due to assignment deadlines it is not always feasible to re-
> serve and await books.

Other comments raised wider issues of time available for the pur-
suit of materials not supplied with the course. For example:

> In general reading lists were received too late to make it
> feasible to get hold of the material without a great deal of
> difficulty.

> Currently I may visit four or five libraries to get the neces-
> sary material.

> The time I expend on accessing information is out of all
> proportion to the level of my studies.

> A lot of time is wasted trying to get access to materials
> which normal students get easily.

> The course I am doing provides additional reading which
> includes pages from suggested books, articles, etc. and has
> cut down on time wasting looking for specific books in
> order to read certain pages.

The idea of time as a commodity which can be spent and wasted
runs throughout these comments. The following comment underlines
the conflict between the demand for longer borrowing periods and the
need to access material quickly:

> . . . I often think that lecturers do not appreciate the time
> involved in choosing/ordering materials which can be sub-
> stantial, even for the initiated, given that materials have to
> be obtained often from elsewhere, or that there is a good
> deal of competition from other students on similar
> courses.

General time pressure
Further references were made to time, 55 in all, which could not be
included in the categories above. From this group of responses, one
gets a feeling for the general pressure under which DL students pursue
their courses. A number of comments referred to pressure or limitation

of time, without making explicit the source of the restriction. However, four major themes emerge from this section of the data:

- time for travel;
- restriction on time due to family commitments;
- restriction on time due to work;
- constraints on time imposed by the course itself.

There seems to be a hierarchy of time pressures, with the same person often being subject to more than one pressure. For example:

> I work full time a fair way from home and am a single parent. With two small children and a full-time job, my time (and money) is limited.

> I work full time, usually 12 hours a day, in a high pressure financial job.

> I work full time. I have a family. I run a large department. I do my course for the pleasure of learning but I do not have the time to mess about waiting for distance library services.

> I have a young family and am a single parent, therefore getting to a library for long enough periods to study on the premises is very difficult as I work as well.

> The main reason I don't use libraries for this course is time—finding time to do the basic course work is difficult enough to do when my wife works full time and when children of 11 and 14 need organizing.

One student summed up the need for well-organized library facilities:

> If you are making a commitment to a course, especially while working full time, library facilities that are accessible, user friendly and understanding of the problems that distance creates are invaluable.

The following comments tend to suggest a perception that course material requires very detailed reading. There is not much evidence in the comments below of an understanding of different levels or approaches to reading, or of the idea of students making selective choices about reading:

> Unfortunately the particular course I am studying is so wordy that it precludes further reading.

> . . . the timetable is so demanding that there is little time left to spend looking for further reading, let alone reading the text. Nice in an ideal world, but in reality the course materials provided are more than enough to work through.

The comments in this section point to a need for training in reading strategies and study skills in general.

Other comments

A number of points (46) could not be included in any of the categories mentioned so far. Of these, four made reference to the importance of the library as a quiet place to work.

> I only used the library as a quiet area to cram before examinations.

> . . . the primary purpose is to find a conducive area in which to study.

A further five made reference to library stock, either praising or complaining of the relevance of stock in the host library:

> Host university library does not hold sufficient material on course topic.

> Do universities who set required reading lists ever check on sorts of numbers of copies of specific reading books?

> The textbooks in xxxx University Library are old and far harder to understand than the issued course books.

Specific courses need use of host university library.

Other points raised include reference to the importance of student initiative in finding materials:

Basically mature, DL students should be resourceful rather than expect too much support . . .

Finally, one student said:

We get the strong impression that they [course providers] are only interested in us as fee providers and are not prepared to consider what services should be made available to us.

Summary of issues

In general the open-ended questions provide evidence for a widespread positive attitude towards using libraries and librarians. The question we asked about manner of treatment at libraries, and which we expected to reveal a good deal of complaint, in fact elicited markedly positive attitudes towards the libraries visited and satisfaction with the way in which students had been treated. Generally, in response to this question, complaint and criticism were prefaced with words of praise and appreciation.

However, this general level of satisfaction with libraries should be seen in relation to a generally low level of expectation regarding what rights and services should be available for DL students. Frequently, students are pleased not to be obviously discriminated against. We have the impression that many students are pleased to be treated 'just like a normal student', or not a source of identifiable nuisance, even if this means a lack of special consideration for the particular difficulties they face.

Students' use of libraries rests heavily on whatever previous experience or training they may have had. If they do not have an undergraduate degree, this experience is likely to be scant. If they achieved a first degree some years ago, they are likely to be out of date regarding developments in new technology. Where training had been received as part of the current programme, it was likely to have been a short introductory talk or guided visit. Only a very small number of students indicated training sessions or programmes of a more extensive nature.

Strikingly, some students feel they lack basic information and training about usual library services. A few students don't even know whether they have any right to use the library at the institution which delivers their course. Many want specific information about the usual range of services a library can offer to 'normal' students. The extent of this elementary training need is in excess of the expressed demand for any remote services, whether postal loans or electronic access.

Where students did make requests for special DL services or arrangements, there was a clear prioritizing of access to a local university library over demand for remote services. Students want access to a nearby library. They are perplexed at the lack of cooperative arrangements between universities, given the minimal use they are able to make of the host library.

The most common category of complaint about library charges concerned the cost of membership or borrowing rights, followed by interlibrary loan. It might be inferred from this that these charges relate to the services of nearby university or specialist libraries, since we have not so far heard of the host library making additional charges to its own students, or of the public library service making other than very small charges for interlibrary loan.

Despite a number of emphatically positive comments about particular courses or services, the 'additional comments' section of the questionnaire overwhelmingly attracted issues of complaint or requests for additional services or training. Here the most frequently raised issues were: the extent of the need for libraries; access to nearby university or other specialist libraries; and pressure of time.

While some students complained that course materials should be all-inclusive so that a library is not needed, almost twice as many stated that this was either impossible or undesirable. Many more comments or requests implicitly acknowledged the importance of library use, with reciprocal arrangements being the most frequently raised issue. The weight of evidence is towards student recognition of the necessity and value of this part of their studies.

While a few students noted the pleasures of library use and found no problems with access, for the vast majority this is an area fraught with difficulties and frustrations. A few were shocked at the difficulties. Comments relating to access to local university or specialist facilities far outweighed the number of comments relating to the host library. While postal services would no doubt be of value to many, students seem to want access to libraries near where they live. Many think it is the responsibility of the course provider to negotiate this. Students want the kind of library access that enables them to browse and make decisions about whether or not to borrow, or whether or not to buy. Many commented on the second class level of access that external membership often gives.

A substantial minority of the sample had special means of access to library facilities. Some worked in universities or other educational institutions. Others worked in businesses with their own library. Some relied on friends, spouses, their own children and professional connections. Often the public library was the only resource. Comments about these disparate arrangements and means of contact had one thing in common: they were frequently viewed by the individual as untypical of the DL students in general. In fact, a broad view of these arrangements suggests that they are typical of the patchwork of provision to which DL students must have recourse. If anything typifies the DL student it is the range and versatility of solutions that they bring to this difficult problem.

One point, raised in connection with specific questions about training, was emphasized again under 'additional comments': more than remote services from the host, our student sample seems to need basic training in what a library can offer. Some lack the most fundamental information about getting a library card from the host library, how a library might fit into their studies, or how to find their way around a catalogue system. These are basic training issues which students on all university courses face. Distance learners often lack these skills because of their previous educational history, or lack of contact with recent developments in library technology. Comments on information technology referred generally to absences of information, training or access. Where the Internet or dial-in services were raised, comments more often showed remote wishes rather than practical knowledge or experience of what was available.

The issue of time was raised with unanticipated persistence. Lack of time was raised as a problematic issue more frequently than distance. For one student, DL was almost synonymous with time pressure. Indeed, the geographical location of many of our students suggests that lack of available time to study by any other means is one of the driving forces behind the growth of DL. Looked at in one way, if students choose DL courses because they are short of time, it is hardly surprising that this should be seen as major constraint in relation to library use.

Several time-related issues were raised: limited library opening times; restrictive loan periods; frustration at the unanticipated time demands in simply getting hold of material, often exacerbated by unsuccessful visits to more than one library. Students seem to be regarding time as a resource or a limited commodity, and the time demands of library access come across as something that they, or perhaps their course providers, had simply not budgeted for. The largest group of time complaints referred to one aspect or another of the student's own situation: high pressure jobs; children to be organized and looked after; working single parents; or families with two full-time wage earners.

A further time-related issue was raised with implications for course design and the training of students. Several students suggested that the course materials themselves were an obstacle to library use. Some students seem to perceive the course material as something which must necessarily be worked through sequentially before additional sources are explored. This is a linear view of learning, suggesting a lack of high level reading skills. It is perhaps symptomatic of the pressing need for more extensive study and information skills training.

Determinants of and barriers to library use

The concern of this section is to tease out the factors which are related to library use. These are divided into 'determinants' and 'obstacles' as a focus for discussion, although it is recognized that this distinction may be only partially supported by the data.

The section draws upon both quantitative and qualitative data generated by the student questionnaire. In dealing with responses to the closed questions the approach differs from that described above in the section on statistically significant relationships (p.57), in that it follows one interpretative path through the data guided by interest in the outcome of extent of library use. In describing this path, data are drawn from the findings presented in that section. In addition, issues arising from the open-ended questions, described in the previous section (p.60), are also drawn upon.

Determinants of library use

Extent of library use was measured in two ways. The questionnaire asked students to indicate whether or not they had used any library facilities for their course, and also to indicate, in response to a further question, how many times they had visited their host university library, their nearest university library, their nearest public library and any specialist library. The first of these questions was aimed at finding out whether there had been any use of a library, whatever library that might be, and however minimal the use. The second question was designed to differentiate between use of the different types of library, and to restrict responses to visits within a three month period. Responses to these questions are combined in the analysis below.

• *Subject area.* Overall, 72.3 per cent of the students had used some kind of library for the purposes of their course. However, this figure conceals some statistically significant differences between subject areas. Table 15 clearly indicates disciplinary differences in the use of libraries. While the general picture seems to be one of extensive use of libraries in all areas, the data suggest some differences in use of libraries between disciplinary areas. Almost all students of Librarianship and Information Science (LIS) have made use of a library, and 98.7 per cent of Education students have done so while the comparative figure for Management students is only 61 per cent.

Table 15: Crosstabulation of whether or not a library has been used against subject areas

	Count Exp Val	SUBJECT				
		Managemnt	Education	LIS	Other	Row Total
LIBRARY USED?	Col Pct	1	2	3	4	
Yes		340	229	77	60	706
		403.7	183.4	56.5	62.3	72.5%
		61.0%	90.5%	98.7%	69.8%	
No		217	24	1	26	268
		153.3	69.6	21.5	23.7	27.5%
		39.0%	9.5%	1.3%	30.2%	
	Column Total	557	253	78	86	974
		57.2%	26.0%	8.0%	8.8%	100.0%

Chi Square probability < .00001

A possible explanation of the less than expected use of libraries by Management students might have been that the sample included students nearer the beginning of their courses in this subject area than in others. However, an inspection of the data shows that this is not the case. On average the Management students had been studying for 24.8 months, while the comparable figures for Education and LIS students are 11.4 and 15.1 months. In fact Education and LIS students were, on average, at an earlier stage of their courses, but were making more use of libraries than the Management group.

Table 16 shows how increasing frequency of library visits is related to subject area. The LIS group shows the greatest discrepancy between observed and expected students making 10 or more visits. A smaller discrepancy is shown for Educational students. By contrast, Management students averaging 10 or more visits are fewer than expected.

Table 16: Crosstabulation of grouped number of visits to any library by subject area

Count Exp Val Row Pct Col Pct	Managemnt	Education	LIS	Other	Row Total
REQUIRED	1	2	3	4	Total
No visits	243	37	11	20	311
	182.0	77.7	27.0	24.3	34.7%
	78.1%	11.9%	3.5%	6.4%	
	46.3%	16.5%	14.1%	28.6%	
1-4 visits	172	92	23	30	317
	185.5%	79.2	27.6	24.7	35.3%
	54.3%	29.0%	7.3%	9.5%	
	32.8%	41.1%	29.5%	42.9%	
5-9 visits	67	63	21	11	162
	94.8	40.5	14.1	12.6	18.1%
	41.4%	38.9%	13.0%	6.8%	
	12.8%	28.1%	26.9%	15.7%	
10 or more visits	42	32	23	9	107
	62.6	26.7	9.3	8.4	11.9%
	40.2%	29.9%	21.5%	8.4%	
	8.2%	14.3%	29.5%	12.9%	
Column Total	525	224	78	70	897
	58.5%	25.0%	8.7%	7.8%	100.0%

Chi-Square probability < .00001
Phi   .34806
Cramer's V   .20095
Number of Missing Observations: 80

- *Course provider expectations* also seem to be unevenly distributed between subject areas. As already noted, there is a mismatch between course provider expectations and student perceptions of the need for library use, with greater numbers of students using libraries than course provider expectations might indicate. Table 17 also suggests that course provider expectations of library use are unevenly distributed between subjects, with only 20.5 per cent of Management students stating that the expectation to use the library has been made clear, compared to 58.8 per cent of Education students and 83.3 per cent of LIS students. This difference mirrors the findings in relation to library use while indicating that there are some courses in Management where there is a clearly stated expectation that libraries be used.

Table 17: Crosstabulation of course provider expectations regarding library use against subject areas

REQUIRED BY COURSE PROVIDER	Count Exp Val Row Pct Col Pct	SUBJECT Managemnt	Education	LIS	Other	Row Total
		1	2	3	4	
yes		115	146	65	42	368
		212.0	94.3	29.5	32.2	37.9%
		31.3%	39.7%	17.7%	11.4%	
		20.5%	58.6%	83.3%	49.4%	
no	2	390	65	7	39	501
		288.6%	128.3	40.2	43.8	51.5%
		77.8%	13.0%	1.4%	7.8%	
		69.6%	26.1%	9.0%	45.9%	
don't know	3	55	38	6	4	103
		59.3	26.4	8.3	9.0	10.6%
		53.4%	36.9%	5.8%	3.9%	
		9.8%	15.3%	7.7%	4.7%	
	Column Total	560 57.6%	249 25.6%	78 8.0%	85 8.7%	972 100.0%

Chi-Square probability < .00001
Number of Missing Observations: 5

- *Age.* There appears to be a small relationship of number of visits to any library with age (Spearman's correlation coefficient: .14; p, .001). Comparison of the age groups shows a small tendency for those aged 40 and over to be making greater use of libraries than those under 40. This finding, however, should be interpreted with caution. Analyzed in this way the data do not show what other intervening variable may affect library use.

- *Stage of course.* There is no statistically significant relationship between length of time of study and number of library visits made. The data fail to confirm the common sense idea that library use becomes more extensive as studies progress towards a dissertation. The view that problems really arise in relation to the dissertation was repeatedly expressed in our discussions with course providers, and the research was approached with the assumption that this would be the case. Some of our student respondents also expressed the same concern in their additional comments. However, as Table 18 shows, there is little variation between the mean number of library visits made by students in years 1, 2 and 3 of their courses.

- *Gender* also shows some relationship to whether or not a visit has been made: 41.4 per cent of male respondents made no library visits, compared to only 26 per cent of females who made no visits, as shown in Table 19. When visits to the different types of library are considered separately, the effect of gender is much reduced, with only visits to specialist libraries showing any significant degree of relationship (Phi = .09502, Chi-square probability < .004). This relationship may be almost entirely due to the use by Librarians of particular specialist libraries, and the overrepresentation of women in this subject area. For other types of library, any gender differences were found to be statistically insignificant.

Table 18: Mean number of visits to any library broken down by length of time the student has been following the course

		N	Mean	Median	Max
YEAR	1 up to 12 months	381	4.0260	2.0	52
YEAR	2 year 2 (13 to 24 mths)	314	4.0637	2.0	58
YEAR	3 year 3	154	4.5909	2.0	70
YEAR	4 year 4	74	5.5270	2.0	85
YEAR	5 year 5	46	3.6957	2.5	53
YEAR	6 year 6	6	3.1667	1.0	9
YEAR	7 year 7	2	1.5000	1.5	2

Total Cases = 977

Table 19: Crosstabulation of sex by no visits or one or more visits to any library

	Count Exp Val Row Pct	no visits	one or more	Row Total
SEX	1	233	330	563
Male		196.6	366.4	58.0%
		41.4%	58.6%	
Female	2	106	302	408
		142.4	265.6	42.0%
		26.0%	74.0%	
	Column Total	339	632	971
		34.9%	65.1%	100.0%

Chi-Square probability with continuity correction = 24.70568
P < .00001
Phi' = .15951

Number of Missing Observations: 6

- *Training.* There is a small but highly significant relationship between having received some training in library use as part of the course and having made one or more visits to all the types of library considered separately and added together. However, out of all the variables considered, training is most closely related to subject of study. This can perhaps be accounted for by the number of professional librarians in the sample. Training also emerged as a key issue in our analysis of open-ended questions. The extent of students' expressed need for the most basic library use training has already been discussed above. Students seem to be working against the odds in making use of libraries without training.

- *Perception of usefulness of material.* One or more visits to the host university library is more likely to have been made if the reading matter in that library is perceived as relatively useful. Similarly, usefulness of material at the nearest university library is positively correlated with having made use of that library. The same kind of relationship exists for public and specialist libraries. However, one observed relationship violates this pattern. There is a correlation between having visited a specialist library and the perception of usefulness of material at the nearest university library, but, in this case, out of those saying that nearest university library material is extremely useful, there is a smaller number than expected who have visited a specialist library. The pattern seems to be of students making some choices about use of libraries rationally related to perceptions of the usefulness of the material they contain.

In the case of the host and the nearest university library, an interesting feature of these relationships is that they seem to be stronger than the effect of distance. Visits to, say, nearby university libraries may be as much conditioned by the belief that they contain useful material as by the fact that they are easier to get to than the host library. Equally, in those cases where students rely on the host library this may be because it contains the kind of collection unavailable elsewhere. From our interviews with DL course providers we know that examples of both these situations exist.

Obstacles to library use

- *Distance.* The scatter diagram in Figure 6 plots miles from host university library against miles from nearest university. While the graph lacks resolution of detail, it gives a feeling for the clustering

Figure 6: Scatter diagram showing miles from host university library in relation to miles from nearest university library

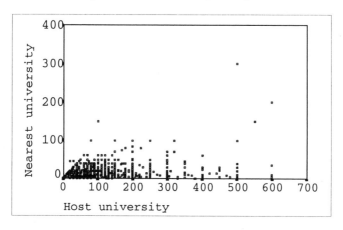

of students relatively close to both, with only a very small minority of students having to travel great distances to the host and the

nearest university. In addition to this, students have access to, and make extensive use of, a public library service which is practically on the doorstep for the vast majority of students. The average estimated travelling time to a public library is 12.6 minutes. Half of the sample live 10 minutes or less from the public library, while 75 per cent live no more than 15 minutes away. Only one respondent indicated a travelling time of more than one hour. While relatively short distances can conceal difficult travelling conditions in urban areas, our survey found strong correlations between distance and estimated travelling time.

Of particular interest is the pattern which emerges when correlations between distance from the host university library and use of the various libraries are examined. A naive assumption might be that distance from the host university library would be inversely related to using that library and positively related to use of other facilities. Indeed, any concern about the overuse of library facilities by students registered at other institutions would need to rest on the idea that these relationships exist. Examination of the data, however, suggests that, while there is a small but statistically significant negative relationship between distance from the host university and frequency of use of its facilities, there is no evidence for any relationship between distance of the host and use of any other facilities. That is, it is apparently *not* the case that registration of students at greater distances is related to increased use of nearby facilities *instead of* those of the host, whether this be a public or a university library.

- *Time.* From analysis of their comments, it is clear that students perceive time to be one of the most important obstacles to library use. If comments about opening times, loan periods and the time it takes to get hold of material are added to comments about work and family pressure, the extent of concern with this issue seems to exceed concern about distance. Students seem to be dismissing use of the host library, and focusing on the time difficulties in making use of nearby facilities. A picture emerges from the comments of the typical student struggling on a tight time budget, and barely managing to make ends meet.

- *Institutional arrangements*. There is a lack of institutional arrangements to facilitate DL students' access to libraries. This absence of arrangements can itself be seen as an obstacle to library use.

Some respondents to the questionnaire did not have any idea of what their rights were in relation to the library of the institution delivering their course. Some made pleas for information, or to be sent a member's ticket. Of our sample, 65.2 per cent said that they had not been sent an information pack about their host university library. A similar proportion is reflected in students' knowledge of how to gain access to a specialist librarian: 54.4 per cent said they did not know how to obtain such access and a further 14.4 per cent were not sure.

Only a small proportion of the sample had used some kind of postal service. While we know of a small number of institutions which offer this kind of service, we believe that much of this proportion would be accounted for by use of professional subscription libraries. In responses to the open-ended questions, comments about postal arrangements almost always referred to their absence.

Of the sample, 58.2 per cent said there is no special arrangement for them to use a university library near where they live. An additional 20.4 per cent did not know whether such an arrangement exists. We know from our survey of university libraries that formal arrangements which do exist are usually geographically restricted, or concern access by the research community, of which masters students are not considered to be a part.

From students' comments it is clear that the lack of reciprocal arrangements to use nearby libraries is a major source of difficulty. When asked how they were treated at the various libraries they used, a frequent response was 'No special DL arrangements'. Students have to negotiate their own access, often pulling whatever strings are available to them, and frequently having to pay a fee for limited access to borrowing rights, interlibrary loan, specialist advice and training. At best such additional fees are an irritant to students who feel they have already subscribed to a library service they cannot use. At worst they deter students from use of a library at all.

A final point about institutional arrangements concerns access for reference purposes. Marginally more of the sample said that they had used libraries for browsing and reading than for borrowing. University libraries traditionally allow free access for reference purposes to the public for *bona fide* reasons. Several respondents complained that reference only access was inadequate to their needs. However, it is worth noting the way in which this traditional freedom to browse can support the activities of adult learners.

Summary of determinants and barriers

The distinction between 'determinants' and 'obstacles' might be seen as an approximation to students' own perceptions of causality. A diagrammatic representation of the factors discussed is presented in Figure 7. The diagram shows the relationship between the student and the library at the centre, with 'barriers' represented as concentric circles and 'determinants' as rays focusing on the centre.

Figure 7: Factors affecting the relationship of DL students to libraries

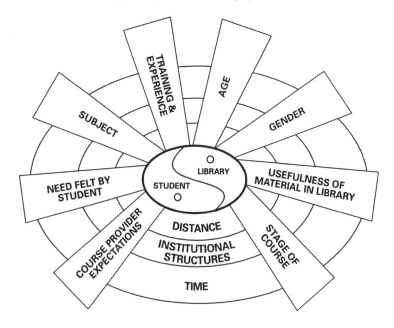

Time, distance and institutional arrangements are perceived by students as major problem categories. There is some evidence, particularly from students' responses to open-ended questions, for such a categorization. However, statistical analysis suggests that distance in itself may not present as great a barrier as might be commonly supposed. In addition, the statistical analysis also suggests that subject, provider expectations, gender, age and usefulness of material interact in complex ways to determine library use. However, some commonly held views are thrown into doubt by the data. Firstly, students are using libraries throughout their courses, not just in preparation for dissertations. Secondly, any apparent effects of age are outweighed by subject and course provider expectations. Thirdly, course provider expectations can cut across views of what is typically expected in a given subject area.

CHAPTER 3

University library survey

Introduction

This chapter presents the findings of a questionnaire survey of higher education libraries in the UK.

Methodology

For this part of our study, we convened a librarians' advisory group comprised of six librarians from a range of 'old' and 'new' universities (including the Open University), and a college of higher education to advise us on the nature, scope and content of this questionnaire. It was made clear to the researchers that librarians in the HE sector would be more willing to cooperate with the survey if they were given adequate opportunities to raise the issues which concerned them about the growth of DL and their relationship with academic departments. In addition, librarians would also want to voice their opinions about administrative and management issues related to the creation and delivery of DL courses in their institutions. The funding arrangements for DL students were seen to be of major significance for librarians and, hence, five questions (7-11) were devoted to this issue.

Whilst librarians were obviously concerned about the ways in which library resources are managed for DL students within their own institutions, they also expressed the hope that the survey might gather much-needed data on the state of reciprocal arrangements for postgraduate DL students throughout the UK. Reciprocal arrangements between HE institutions vary throughout the UK but are generally seen to have broken down since the ending of the binary divide between universities and polytechnics in 1992. We decided, therefore, to divide the questionnaire into three sections: the first section to cover questions related to the design and delivery of DL courses within the librarian's own institution; the second section to cover questions about whether and how that institution was involved in any reciprocal arrangements with other institutions; and the third section to provide space for additional comments. The librarians who advised us on the design of the questionnaire felt that the third section was important as some librarians might have useful examples to report of good practice in their own institutions, or they might wish to raise general policy or practice-related points about the growth of DL and its implications for HE libraries.

As a considerable amount of time was devoted to this consultation exercise, it was not felt necessary to pilot the questionnaire before it was distributed. The final version of the questionnaire was approved by the librarians' advisory group who ensured that the language used was appropriate and included the everyday terminology of the profession.

The questionnaire was distributed to the 158 librarians of HEFC funded institutions. Of these, 116 were returned, giving a response rate of 73.4 per cent. A copy of the questionnaire is reproduced in Appendix 3.

Quantitative findings

Design and delivery of DL courses within institution

This section covers part A, questions 1 to 20, of the questionnaire. Over half of the librarians (52.3 per cent) reported that their institution had some involvement in the provision of postgraduate DL courses. Table 20 indicates the percentage of those running such courses for named subject areas. The second column of figures indicates the percentage planning named courses in each subject area.

The most common discipline areas to have DL courses, as reported by librarians in this survey, were Business and Management (53.2 per cent) and Education (46.9 per cent) with the third highest being Social Sciences (34.5 per cent). DL courses were being planned in every discipline listed in the questionnaire, with the biggest growth areas likely to be Social Sciences and subjects and professions allied to Medicine.

Just under two-thirds of institutions (61.7 per cent) reported that their DL students normally register with the library of the host institution. The majority of libraries (78 per cent) do not distinguish between DL students and other part-time students. The average

Table 20: Involvement in provision of postgraduate DL courses for named subject areas

Subject Area	Current	Planned
Clinical and Pre-Clinical Subjects	9.1	3.6
Subjects and Professions Allied to Medicine	21.2	11.5
Science	15.4	1.9
Engineering and Technology	25.4	5.1
Built Environment	17.0	0
Mathematical Sciences, IT and Computing	20.7	8.6
Business and Management	53.2	9.7
Social Sciences	34.5	10.3
Humanities	14.8	5.6
Art, Design and Performing Arts	3.8	1.9
Education	46.9	3.1

estimated number of DL students registered at host university libraries was 222, with the maximum estimated number being 1,000.

Just under two-thirds of the libraries (62.5 per cent) reported that DL students are funded on a *per capita* basis at the same rate as other part-time students and 86.8 per cent reported that their library did not receive a lower level of funding for DL students as compared to other part-time students.

The vast majority of libraries (91.7 per cent) did not receive ear-marked or ring-fenced funding for DL students, and nor did the majority (88.3 per cent) receive funds for the provision of experimental or additional services for DL students. An 'old' university in Scotland that does allocate some of its funding for DL students, reported that, 'Special funding would allow us to be more pro-active/experimental'.

It is notable that whilst just over two-thirds of libraries (67.8 per cent) reported that they were consulted about the resource implications of new DL courses, a similar number (63.2 per cent) reported that they were not involved in the planning of new courses. This suggests that, currently, the majority of course designers have a largely functional and limited view of the role of librarians *vis-à-vis* DL courses. Hence, librarians are asked to comment on resource implications, introduce students to the library and provide training in information skills and generally assist students. Librarians are not, on the whole, regarded as members of course teams or given a role in course evaluation.

Just under one-third of librarians (32.1 per cent) reported having an involvement in IT projects designed to provide students with remote access facilities. This is surprising, given the growth of initiatives in this area, but possibly reflects the limited nature of the relationship between academic course providers and librarians. If librarians were fully involved in the development and design of DL courses, they might both instigate IT initiatives and play a much bigger role in the setting-up of such initiatives in their institutions.

The vast majority of libraries (81.8 per cent) did not have a specialist DL librarian and in the cases of those that did, only 3.4 per cent reported that it was a full-time responsibility. Two institutions reported that they employ one full-time DL librarian; one reported employing three DL librarians; and one reported employing four DL librarians.

Table 21 shows the range of services which the libraries indicated that they offered to DL students. Although significant numbers of libraries reported that they offer a wide range of services to DL students, just under two-thirds (61.4 per cent) do not provide a leaflet informing students of these services. Just over two-thirds of libraries (68.4 per cent) reported that they will send articles by post to students and just under half (49.1 per cent) reported that they post books to students in the UK. These figures seem to be surprisingly high, but it should be remembered that they reflect an intention rather than any formal arrangements for postal services. If a student asks for an article or book to be posted, it seems that a large number of libraries will respond positively, but there are very few examples of libraries which have established postal services available to all DL students and advertised as such.

The responses to this question suggest that, for most of the listed services, over half of the libraries are attempting to respond to DL students' needs but there are still significant numbers which do not provide any services. None of the libraries reported that they had discontinued any services for DL students.

Physical access to libraries is, however, a problem for DL students as over two-thirds (77 per cent) of libraries reported that they did not open at special times, for example to coincide with residential weekends.

Table 21: Services offered to DL students

Service	Yes
	%
A leaflet describing services to distance learning students	38.6
Telephone catalogue enquiries	88.1
Telephone renewals	93.4
Telephone reservations	66.1
24 hour answer phone	18.6
Freephone service	0
Response to fax	74.1
Response to email	74.1
Longer loan periods or renewals	31.6
Special collection of books	15.0
Literature searches requested from a distance	63.2
Sending searches on disc	25.0
Photocopying articles requested by students	58.6
Sending articles by post	68.4
Sending books by post within the UK	49.1
Freepost return within UK	0
Sending books by post outside UK	14
Access to JANET from home computer	55.6

Reciprocal arrangements with other institutions

This section covers part B, questions 24 to 33, of the questionnaire. Just under two-thirds of libraries (63 per cent) reported that they allowed all DL students from any other institutions to use their facilities for reference purposes. A further 28.7 per cent said they allowed access in some circumstances, and 8.3 per cent said they did not allow access. Taking these latter totals together, one-third of libraries restricted or denied access to their facilities to DL students from other institutions.

The responses to question 24 need to be considered in the light of the answers to question 26 in which the majority of libraries (78.3 per cent) said they did participate in the book purchasing agreement which allows *bona fide* members of the public to use their facilities for reference purposes without charge.

Several libraries reported that they have reciprocal arrangements with a range of universities for postgraduate research students and academic staff only. (Further comment on these arrangements is provided below.) In a small number of cases, reciprocal arrangements appear to cover all students and so would include those studying by DL. It should be noted, however, that the picture is very confused. In some cases, for example, different institutions were named as being part of the same reciprocal arrangements. In other cases, the comment about such arrangements would include *caveats* such as 'I think this is the case', or 'I suspect that students would have to make prior arrangements to make the system work'.

Some reciprocal arrangements reflect the way in which library collections complement each other. For example, the Royal Veterinary College in London has reciprocal arrangements with the National Institute for Biological Sciences and the University of London libraries. These arrangements may also reflect a partnership between a group of institutions which are geographically very close. For example, CALIM (Consortium of Academic Libraries in Manchester) covers the University of Manchester, the University of Manchester Institute of Science and Technology, the Manchester Business School, and Manchester Metropolitan University. In Canterbury, the University of Kent and Christchurch College allow each other's students to have limited borrowing rights but students have to make individual applications. In Scotland, the Agreement of the Scottish Federation of Universities and Research Libraries gives students reference access and private study rights at Aberdeen, Dundee, Abertay, Edinburgh, Glasgow, Glasgow Caledonian, Heriot-Watt, Napier, Paisley, St. Andrews, Stirling and Robert Gordon Universities.

As well as being confused and complex, reciprocal arrangements can also be strained. For example, one 'older' university has withdrawn from the partnership between university libraries in Yorkshire, and currently expects an exchange of finance for use by staff and research students of other institutions in the region. A member of the London Plus scheme which provides reciprocal links between 12 university libraries (11 'new' and one 'old') commented:

> [London Plus] is generally a good thing. In practice, however, we do not encourage much use of our libraries (13 in all) as they are mutually far apart (e.g. three miles) and in heavy demand from campus-based students.

This problem of achieving a balance was highlighted by the University College of St. Martin's in Lancaster which reported that it has students in Carlisle who want to make use of libraries in Glasgow,

Edinburgh and Newcastle. St. Martin's recognizes, however, that students in those Universities would not, necessarily, have much call on its library.

A small minority of libraries (5.9 per cent) reported that they could not cope with the level of demand from DL students, whilst just under two-thirds (64.4 per cent) said they could manage.

Just under half the libraries (45.1 per cent) reported that DL students from other institutions could purchase external borrower status from them, whilst just under one-third (30.4 per cent) did not allow this and 24.5 per cent did so but only in some circumstances. One 'old' English university reported that it would grant external borrower status 'in special circumstances' and gave as an example 'if the student could demonstrate they had a disability'. Some universities stipulated that they required authorization from the student's tutor before granting external borrower status.

Table 22 lists the services to which reciprocal arrangements and/or external borrower status gives DL students access. It is clear from this table that reciprocal arrangements only account for a minority of the provision for DL students. In the main, if DL students want access to services at a library other than the one at their host institution, they will have to pay not only a fee for external borrower status but, in some cases, an additional cost for each individual service they require.

Table 22: Access to services for DL students through reciprocal arrangements and external borrower status

Service	Reciprocal Arrangement	External Borrower	Additional Charge
	%	%	%
Reservations	7.9	54.0	1.6
Borrowing for same periods as your own students	12.3	47.4	0
Borrowing for restricted periods or items	7.9	39.5	0
Induction to the library	12.5	31.3	6.3
Information skills training	7.1	14.3	42.9
Services of specialist librarian	17.8	24.4	11.1
Access to OPAC	11.2	28.1	50.0
Use of CD-ROM on stand alone machine	15.3	37.3	3.4
Access to networked databases	6.3	25.0	12.5
Access to BIDS	15.4	30.8	7.7
Interlibrary Loan	4.4	4.4	60.0

The majority of libraries (82.2 per cent) did not currently have electronic barriers in place for checking membership on entry but 17.8 per cent did and a further 20.9 per cent were planning to introduce barriers in 1996. By now, therefore, over a third of libraries (40 per cent) will have introduced electronic barriers.

Responses to open-ended questions

The comments provided in response to the open-ended questions in part C of the questionnaire have been presented and summarized under five headings which reflect the key areas of concern for university librarians when considering their relationship to DL students and DL courses:

- reciprocal arrangements: theory and practice;
- library/academic communication and liaison;
- DL students' needs;
- staffing and resource issues;
- future developments.

Reciprocal arrangements: theory and practice

The majority of university libraries stated that effective and fair reciprocal arrangements must be developed but also noted that current arrangements, where they exist, are *ad hoc* and piecemeal:

> [Access to HE library is] valuable for hands-on experience, and developing information skills: something DLs can miss out on if they rely on a remote library. However, we have reciprocal arrangements with few libraries. Some academic libraries don't allow access as a matter of policy. Not all students live near an appropriate library. Students may not be allowed access to databases/electronic information sources due to licensing arrangements.

There were voices of caution, stressing that whilst such arrangements were fine in theory, there was a problem for those institutions which turned out to be 'net' providers. There needs to be a balance between levels of demand and supply.

Some institutions were said to be becoming 'protectionist' and so generally opposed to reciprocal arrangements. Such a situation reflects the competitive climate in which HE is having to operate. The following comment from an 'old' university in England indicates that some university libraries may only just be realizing that their services are being used by DL students:

> Our policies re. visitors and external users have been very lax. We need to tighten up and allow use only from institutions with which we have reciprocal arrangements which benefit our students.

A further problem with reciprocal arrangements is that a host university cannot and should not assume that an institution close to its students' homes will have adequate collections for the courses in question. There is an irony here for, if such an assumption could be made, then those local institutions ought to be running the same courses and, therefore, DL might not be necessary.

The following comments reflect the irritation expressed by some respondents at what they regard as irresponsible behaviour by course providers who, in not providing adequate library access for their students, are charged with providing a sub-standard educational service for their own students and endangering the quality of service available to other students.

> The number of such students requesting access is increasing. It is irritating that in 99 per cent of cases the home university has made no attempt to ensure that library services are in place, and one wonders about the internal validation of courses in such circumstances—although, of course, that also applies to the leader in the field, the OU.

> Distance learning is a praiseworthy concept. Some of the students, however, and perhaps some of their institutions, expect other libraries to open their doors to distance learners. The home institution receives funds for distance learners and they cannot expect other libraries to provide services at no cost.

> [Reciprocal arrangements are] currently extremely limited and of negative value, [and so] the demand is likely to be

unpredictable and damaging to the availability of materials
for home students. It creates a specious justification for
institutions to evade their responsibility to provide required materials. It encourages the irresponsible acceptance of students onto courses who, it is quite clear, will
never gain the level of access to materials required for a
good learning experience.

. . . I would add that it is a delusion, and a wilful one at
that, that reciprocal access to materials will solve the resourcing problems of distance students. It is entirely arbi-
trary which institution a distance student will find
themselves in proximity to, and the profile of stock is
likely to be quite inappropriate. Stock profiles are the result of close liaison with academic departments, as is the
service provided by libraries, and needs to be to give
students good value. You will always be able to get distance students through exams using the methods perfected
at 'A' level and with the Open University, namely make
sure that they have only the data that they will have to re-
produce in an exam. The quality of learning will remain
shabby at best, which is not to say that the students will be
any poorer than any others. I understand and sympathize
with extending opportunities to students who are isolated
and immobile. That does not prevent me from believing
that such educational experience is very poor.

To organize and establish reciprocal arrangements at both local and
national levels, librarians stressed that senior academics and vice-
chancellors have to lead the way. This important strategic development has to have firm leadership and should not be left to librarians,
as the following comment makes clear:

Value [of reciprocal arrangements] is inhibited by reluc-
tance of regular users to travel. Net providers are not
compensated. In my experience library cooperation of this
kind requires academic cooperation and strong leadership
by vice chancellors. Library initiated arrangements usually
run into opposition in the institution which is the net
provider.

Further comments emphasize the need for national arrangements to be made, given the changing nature of the student body in HE in which part-time and mature students are featuring more and more prominently.

> There is a need for a national policy which would extend beyond distance education. For example, in vacation periods other part-time students and also full-time students require access to libraries at institutions other than their home institution. It is of vital importance to all students, but particularly to those in distance education, that libraries cooperate nationwide in making available the resources needed to support their studies.

> Reciprocal arrangements are becoming increasingly important, given the increase in distance of students, whether formal DL or not. Currently market forces are prevailing. Increasingly arrangements will/must be made with institutions other than HE, e.g. commerce, industry and government departments.

> Distance Learning is a growth area for academic institutions. We need to allocate time to plan how to support the student, and market the library so departments running such courses are aware of the role the library has in making the courses a success or failure.

Library/academic communication and liaison

Many librarians cited the lack of adequate communication and liaison with academic departments as a major source of irritation and frustration when it came to trying to find solutions to meeting the needs of DL students. Librarians feel they are often 'left in the dark' about DL developments and that course providers do not spend enough time considering the library needs of their students. The following comment from an 'old' university in England reflects this:

> We don't know who they [DL students] are, how many are being recruited and what services they think they can get. There seems to be no general University policy on distance learners. Arrangements are departmental and

therefore *ad hoc* . . . This is a topic of concern here. We
are very uncertain as to how to offer library services to
distance learners. The University needs to get its own act
together and we are pressing for this. What is certain is
that these students need library services of some sort and
also need library/information retrieval skills. Very often
the first we know of their needs is when they ask us to
provide something that we cannot do. This gives us a
feeling of inadequacy and is of no support to the student.
Helping them will require extra resources, both in stock
and staff and we need to bid for these.

In contrast, liaison with course providers has led two respondents
to take the view that DL courses should be self-contained, thereby
removing the problem of library access and use:

Students on our one DL course receive a study pack with
lecture notes, articles and chapters for each module, which
the course organizer feels is reasonably sufficient.

The largest DL programme run here . . . operates with the
explicit aim of providing all students with all the material
they will need, so that whatever local resources they might
or might not have access to, and wherever they live, they
have the same learning experience and opportunities. This
seems to me a laudable aim for all DL courses.

These views would appear to be unrepresentative, however, as several
respondents expressed the view that DL students were entitled to have
access to adequate library facilities. Some respondents linked the
problems faced by DL students to the needs of part-time students in
general and stressed that libraries would have to develop strategies to
cater for such students. The following comment summarizes these
views and begins by highlighting the ambiguous definition of the term
'DL':

Definitions of DL [are] not precise. We have no formal
DL courses, but do have students living at considerable
distance and they bring many of the same problems. Most
library systems do not cater adequately for such individuals as they have to be organized for the majority. We are

certainly aware of the conflict and the questions, but not yet the answers! However, since it seems certain that this will be a major development in education we will have to change, as it seems likely that funding will also change, to reflect a new reality.

DL students' needs

Several respondents identified DL students as having specific needs, highlighted in particular in these comments:

> Provision should endeavour to recognize that DL students are in most cases getting their study around job and family commitments. They may need access to library resources at all times of day, night and throughout the year; often at times when library provision to full-time students is restricted. DL students are also characterized by having very different levels of access to learning resources and facilities. Compare this with relatively uniform access which can be provided to all the students on a full-time course. Library provision for DL students is not yet taking full advantage of networking technologies. Proper provision for DL students has significant costs for libraries but these are different in nature to the costs of servicing full-time students.

> . . . Library provision for DL students is essential. However, from experience (being a distance learner myself) library services available to students are often under promoted or not promoted at all. All students need to feel part of the university they attend. They require information as efficiently and effectively as possible.

Some librarians, however, whilst being aware of the particular needs of DL students also point out that these students can sometimes exert considerable pressure on library services. Such students tend to see themselves as 'customers' who have paid fees and expect to be provided with the services they require to complete their courses. In some cases, DL students may be in a position to ask secretaries or other support staff in their workplaces to contact libraries on their behalf as the following respondent indicates:

> Many DL students are based in industry where they may
> have the support of information officers, who may process
> the information rather than just finding it . . . Should we
> be liaising with these company information staff? It is not
> the task of the librarian to do the project work—some
> students forget this.

The very fact that most DL students are also in full-time employment and have domestic responsibilities which are typical for part-
time students in general, means that they have little time to waste.
Their sense of urgency can have a widespread impact on library staff
as this respondent illustrates:

> DL learners put great strain on library services. A: Need
> books from a reading list—books not normally in our
> library, so we have to buy or get ILL. B: Need things im-
> mediately—they normally travel a long way to the library.
> Need things last minute—normally to meet project dead-
> lines. C: Need lots of support in CD training, etc., and are
> normally very adept at putting pressure on library staff
> (because they have to because of their situation) to do
> searches for them. D: Difficult to get books back because
> they don't visit the library often. Books therefore circulate
> more slowly. E: Generally are very stressed and need
> more time from the librarian (*in loco* tutor!)

Staffing and resource implications

The majority of respondents referred to staffing and resource problems as being the key obstacles to improving services for DL students.
The following comments indicate that improvements will only be
possible if there are considerable shifts in terms of working patterns,
awareness of students' needs and the allocation of central university
resources.

> We have generous opening hours but no professional-
> level staff employed out of normal teaching hours—this
> can be disadvantageous to part-time or DL students.

> Employment of casual staff to support extended opening
> (training, supervision, communication issues).

The main obstacle is the recognition by senior management in the institution that such development is expensive in terms of staff time and resources.

Main problem is of resource—i.e., no real problem if visiting student merely wants to consult a journal/book, but limited space available for study purposes (own students take precedence); insufficient equipment to allow visiting students access to online, CD-ROM; insufficient staff and time to provide detailed guidance to finding information.

Weekend opening particularly [for] multi-site libraries is very expensive. We are currently exploring ways of improving our weekend hours for the benefit especially of part-time (and DL) students.

Done on goodwill of staff involved. In general we now employ a separate team of staff to staff opening hours in the evening and weekends which brings issues of different levels of service available at different times and lots of training issues.

Lack of resources to provide specific services for DL students, e.g. postal loans, reservations, photocopying, librarians dedicated to DL students.

DL students are certainly a special category of library users and do make additional demands on time and other resources. However, apart from posting library material to them (which we sometimes do for pre-service students as well) the services offered to them are available to all other students, and library staff help them all in the same way. In fact the ITE students are increasingly moving to independent guided study and their needs will overlap more with those of DLs. Libraries in teacher education institutions—and in HE in general—must come to terms with DL and find a suitable balance between serving on and off campus students. At present we are coping with loans to, and reservations for, DLs while using a manual issue system and card catalogue. Certain of the problems will be made much easier when we acquire an automated library system (in 1996, it is hoped). The only standard of performance which we apply at the moment is to try to deal with any DL's enquiry within 24 hours of receipt. We may not always complete the work required in that time, but we always aim to send something, even it's just a message to report progress, by then.

Currently weekend/late night opening is operated on minimal staffing levels with only basic services available. Staff would not be present in sufficient number, or with appropriate expertise, to provide the type of services DL students might expect. Such students can devour staff time—they cannot be present to do things for themselves, they cannot attend routine workshops or training sessions that are run so must rely more on staff help.

We have found that DL students cause us more and more problems as their numbers increase. We have plans to treble our numbers with which we will be unable to cope in terms of staff and finance. As they are all involved in MA in Education work the strain of so many borrowers on our bookstock will become acute. This is coupled with our extra long loan period for DL students. As they all do virtually one course cooperation between students is essential. At the moment our numbers for cooperation are at a finite point, the planned expansion will make this very difficult.

Pilot scheme—provision of individualized services is staff intensive. We hope this will be an interim measure until the 'dial-in' facilities make it possible for all students to answer many of their queries themselves, plus electronic provision of key texts/articles, etc. Additional vacation opening—many staff contracts are term-time only. Full-time staff have to do any overtime needed and take time off in lieu of payment in the summer vacation. It is difficult to man the library even for the traditional vacation opening (especially in the summer). College is unwilling to pay for additional staffing. The problem is brought up at every conceivable committee. The library staff are unwilling to forfeit their leave entitlement.

Future developments

The potential for new technologies to solve some of the problems faced by DL students was referred to by several respondents. For example:

> Access to both libraries and materials is a major issue. How long this will remain so will depend on the rate at which more materials/services become available electronically, and the development of a national infrastructure for electronic networks. Document delivery—the problems surrounding this at present may be eased by new technology—electronic delivery systems for an increasing amount of material, together with electronic journals, as these become more numerous. Instruction and guidance— the student's home institution should provide some guidance in the use of information sources integrated with the course materials. New technology may be used to make more material readily available nationally, across networks, including end-user training materials for both electronic and traditional sources.

> The University now has a Distance Learning Working Party with representation from the Library. Various approaches are being tried including video-conferencing to increase scope of courses delivered at a distance.

> Distance learning students will be a topic of future exploration and networking technology interests us in terms of its power and sophistication. Would need to rethink: (i) loan rules for short loan collection; (ii) sending items by post; (iii) performing cost generating tasks without a signature. Lack of time and other resources.

Two universities offered their vision of how strategies for supporting DL students might be developed. It is worth noting that both involve librarians, course providers and other stakeholders working together:

The University has recently established a DL Forum. The constitution of this is: all course leaders for DL courses, Student Association President, myself, member of the Academic Standards Committee. This is putting DL very much on the map. A lack of awareness of DL students had resulted in library provision being very much minimalized for them. I noticed this and changed their borrowing privileges to reflect those of the full-time student—as they are all fully matriculated students of the university. I think the whole concept of DL and library provision has not been taken on board by the University and it is a huge injustice to these students. The DL Forum is to be lobbying the University to request additional funding for support services (such as library provision) on behalf of all DL students. I support the Forum fully.

The library has set up a DL Initiative to establish methods of delivering information to students in other formats than on paper, to increase the level of interactivity with materials by use of hypertext links and links to resources, to utilize those currently offered by electronic information, to provide greater access to materials and to exploit transnational study networks. The project has partners within the University and will pilot the initiative with two faculties who have a number of DL courses in place. It is intended that the outcomes will include an increase in the number of students able to access courses, a transnational electronic support and information systems for staff and students together with enriched course and support materials. Students who have access to a modem are able to dial into the library catalogue and BIDS source.

Conclusion

This survey indicates that for the majority of HE libraries, servicing the needs of DL students is a growing problem. A diverse range of practices and beliefs has developed, and it is not surprising, therefore, that students often feel confused and uncertain of the services that can be available to them. There is an urgent need for a national strategy and for communicating to students a set of guidelines for access to university libraries.

CHAPTER 4

Survey of public libraries

Introduction

Background research for this project, along with evidence supplied by our student diarists, suggested that postgraduate DL students were making significant use of public libraries. The student questionnaire revealed that, on average, students can reach a public library in less than 15 minutes. The findings presented here from a survey of 134 public libraries in the UK confirm the evidence from the student survey that these libraries are indeed a major resource for students to the extent that the librarians who work in this sector see themselves as providing an 'invisible subsidy to the expansion of higher education'.

Methodology

In order to explore the role of public libraries in postgraduate DL, we decided to survey a sample of libraries by questionnaire (reproduced in Appendix 4). We selected our sample on the basis that:

- those libraries which classify themselves as 'Central' have responsibility for monitoring the work of several branches and should be able to speak from the perspective of public library provision across a wide area;
- given that students revealed they used a mixture of libraries, including very small branch libraries, we included in the sample all of the libraries identified by students in the diary study;
- geographical spread was important, given that local authority funding of libraries differs across the country and the organization of library provision differs from one authority to the next.

Our sample comprised, therefore, the following:

- a main or Central library for each of the 173 areas listed in the Library Association's directory (Harrold, 1993);
- a further 54 branch libraries used by students in the diary study.

Overall the sample includes 80 libraries (both Central and Branch) identified as useful in their studies by the 40 students involved in our diary study.

The questionnaire was designed in consultation with local public librarians who provided very helpful advice about the wording of particular questions and the overall scope of the survey. Recognizing the increasing pressures on public librarians who are facing stringent budget cuts, we decided to restrict the questionnaire to two sides of A4 paper. Overall, 138 responses were received, giving a response rate of 60.8 per cent.

Quantitative findings

The vast majority of public libraries (84 per cent) do not distinguish in their records those users who are students. The figure is even higher (99.2 per cent) for postgraduate DL students. A small minority (1.5 per cent) of libraries had carried out user surveys to identify post-graduate DL students and their needs.

The majority of general students were recorded as being extensive users of public libraries by 72.2 per cent of respondents to this question. Although most libraries do not formally distinguish between types of student, this question still reveals that DL students are seen to be using public libraries to some extent or extensively by 44.7 per cent of the respondents, while 48.5 per cent reported that part-time students were using their libraries extensively.

A range of services which would be of relevance to postgraduate DL students is offered in around half of the libraries in this sample, and nearly all the libraries (98.5 per cent) provide an interlibrary loan service, as indicated by Table 23. There is, however, a significant gap in provision when it comes to access to Online Public Access Cata-logues (OPACs), as one-third of the libraries in the sample (33.1 per cent) did not currently provide this.

The majority of respondents (71 per cent) reported that their stock would be of limited use to postgraduate DL students, while 21.4 per cent saw it as being completely inadequate. Only 4.6 per cent reported that they had a large academic stock.

Table 23: Services offered by public libraries which are of relevance to postgraduate DL students

Service	%
Information about distance learning courses	94.7
A collection of distance learning materials	42.5
Library skills training	52.8
Training in use of bibliographic resources	27.9
Specialized literature searches	42.6
Public access to CD-ROM databases	52.0
Interlibrary loans service	98.5

The majority of public libraries (84.6 per cent) charged £1 or less for interlibrary loan (ILL), with 60p being the average charge. A minority (7.9 per cent) quoted charges of over £1, with £5 being the largest figure. A similar proportion (7.5 per cent) offered the service free. This suggests that charges for interlibrary loans in public libraries are considerably lower than those in university libraries. A Central librarian in Scotland commented that he was finding:

> . . . increasing evidence of use of ILL loans in preference to own college or university. I find this a worrying trend.

A Central librarian in Manchester commented:

> Problems encountered when students try to take advantage of cheap (to them) ILL service in public library, requesting large numbers of obscure items, instead of using appropriate academic library (with much more realistic reservation fee).

The vast majority of public libraries (90.6 per cent) did not have part of their budgets reserved for students in general, and the figure rose to 97.6 per cent in the case of postgraduate DL students. In many cases, respondents made some reference to having their own budgets cut, causing them to reduce their overall level of service to the general public. Some libraries had received extra funding from government via local Training and Enterprise Councils but this was to establish and develop services targeted at disadvantaged groups, notably women returners and the unemployed.

Those libraries which service the needs of geographically remote communities had particular cause to regret the lack of adequate funding for DL students, as this librarian from the Western Islands of Scotland commented:

> Distance learning is common and essential to many, especially in the islands, so public libraries have a responsibility as with any other group in the community, but perhaps more so in the more remote communities where people have restricted opportunities to make alternative arrangements. The reality of public library funding must be fully recognized and appreciated.

Qualitative findings: responses to open-ended questions

In this section we bring together the responses to the open-ended questions under five headings which encapsulate the way in which public librarians appear to be conceptualizing their concerns about the role they play *vis-à-vis* postgraduate DL students:

- equality of opportunity;
- gateways: resources and capability;
- place to study;
- attractiveness of public library;
- student expectation, initial training and preparedness.

Equality of opportunity

The vast majority of public librarians stated that they want to be able to service the needs of DL students and that such students have the right to expect service from their local public library and should be able to exercise that right just as any other member of the public. This is a matter of equality of opportunity. There is, however, a serious problem of under-funding which has caused many of the libraries in the survey to cut back on their level of service and to reconsider the extent to which they can meet people's needs, regardless of their categorization.

Approximately one-third of the libraries referred to their role as 'university of the people' or 'university of the ordinary citizen', by which they meant that they had a duty to ensure that local people, who are not registered students, had access to a library in which they could continue their education. It was the view of these libraries that registered students ought to be catered for by their host universities and should not have to rely on public libraries. It should be added, however, that these libraries would not turn students away as they still believed in the overriding sense of providing a service to local people, as mentioned earlier. The following comment from a County library in Southern England reflects these concerns:

> If public libraries cannot do this, who can? Academic libraries often discourage 'public' access and are often inaccessible to many users. The public library has often and for many years been referred to as 'The University of the People' and in my view this is a much more appropriate use of public library funds than the issuing of pulp fiction or entertainment videos.

Whilst libraries were keen that progress should be made towards the establishment of meaningful reciprocal arrangements, some expressed caution about any move to establish procedures which singled out DL students. If DL students are to be regarded as 'special cases' then they may end up disadvantaged, by having their rights restricted and bound within very formal structures. Again, the point was made that public libraries should be able to offer services to anyone who walks in and not have to begin categorizing people. The following comment from a Central library in Northern Ireland reflects this concern:

> . . . a very strong and supportive role, but I would be wary of a complex structure of formal support. Public libraries can, and should, act as a university library for DL. In this regard I would make little distinction between DL and unregistered or personal learning. The automatic source of material to which many students turn is their local public library. Public libraries have such a wide access criteria that all DL students' needs should fall within the normal established practice for a public library. I believe that to separate students with a separate book fund or separate tickets would be to disadvantage them and to suggest that they do not have a full right to use the library services, or

to request that material be purchased or obtained to meet their needs. I remember very clearly the early complicated instructions for dealing with the first OU students and the quiet dismantling of these schemes within a few years and this has, perhaps, coloured my views. I would suggest that we should make a clear statement of a commitment, urge awarding and providing institutions to inform their students with regard to the services of public library. Public libraries should be in contact with WEAs, educational guidance centres, community education tutors and other persons who may be in touch with DL students to ensure that they are aware of the services of the public library.

Gateways: resources and capability

Most public libraries recognized that they did not hold the types of collections required to meet the needs of postgraduate students and would need increased funding to provide even the most basic IT facilities for DL students. Where public libraries did feel they could play an important role, however, is in acting as a 'gateway' for students by pointing them in the right direction so that they can find the materials they need in other collections. If money were available for IT, public libraries would benefit from having access to JANET at affordable cost and the facilities to network at regional level.

A central problem for public libraries in relation to DL students is time. Whilst they can locate and acquire many of the items requested by students, this material can take a long time to arrive.

Where public libraries had set up open learning centres/spaces and collections, these tended to be related to the needs of people seeking work and/or job-related training.

Place to study

Several libraries noted that they played an important role for DL students by acting as a convenient place in which students could study. For some students, the library provided peace and quiet with friendly staff who were on hand to offer support when necessary.

This recognition of the fact that DL students, in common with part-time students in general, may not have access, at home or at work, to the type of space which is appropriate for studying, reflects a deep understanding on the part of public librarians of their users' needs and lifestyles. In addition, it shows the commitment which these librarians have made to supporting the needs of adult learners.

Attractiveness of public library

Public libraries were aware that they may be providing a cheaper service to students than that offered by university libraries, particularly for interlibrary loan. This had meant an increase in the number of traditional, non-DL students, and in some cases university staff, using the public libraries close to their universities or lodgings. In addition, some libraries noted that their systems were easier to use than those of their neighbouring universities and that they placed fewer restrictions on students.

Student expectation, initial training and preparedness

Librarians cited the lack of adequate training which DL students receive in library and information retrieval skills. This led to many students having unrealistic expectations of the level and nature of the service which public libraries could provide. If students were given appropriate training at the start of their course, this would ease some of the burden on public librarians. While just over half (52.8 per cent) could offer some library skills training to users, very few gave details of any systematic training. One exception is East Surrey Libraries which offer induction courses as a regular service to OU students.

Librarians believed there is a considerable amount of scope for meeting students' needs but this depends on an adequate dialogue between student and librarian. Where students are able to articulate their needs and have some sense of how the library operates, then the librarian can, more easily, begin to find ways of helping the individual.

Students would be better prepared for discussions with librarians if they came armed with adequately prepared reading lists giving complete references for texts. Course providers with large numbers of students could also consider supplying public libraries close to the homes of their DL students with lists of set texts.

Conclusion

This survey demonstrates the important, and largely hidden, role played by public libraries in the lives of postgraduate DL students.

Despite serious financial problems and a recognition that their stock may be only of limited use, public librarians are supporting DL students in a number of significant ways. The following comments, firstly from a Central library in the South East of England, and secondly from a Central library in the English Midlands, reflect the concern of many in the survey and highlight the complexities surrounding the current situation.

> We know this sort of student appreciates our library service, but our funding and resources do not always meet demand. Yes, we are willing to give as much support as we are able. The public library is a readily accessible resource for students. The future, however, is gloomy. Financial resources and numbers of staff are diminishing, opening hours are shortening and some libraries are likely to close. Local government reform will exacerbate these trends, and smaller library authorities will be less able to cope.

> Public libraries have a major role to play in supporting lifelong education. However, we do not aim to provide academic material to postgraduate level. This puts pressure on our inter-loans service and budget. The proliferation of DL courses is beginning to cause us problems. Colleges and universities expect us to support students in growing numbers—this at a time of severe cutbacks in funding. It may well be that as pressures increase there will have to be reductions in the inter-loans/BL service or specific additional charges. More planning/thought/co-operation between all concerned is vital.

Response to this question shows that concern for the adult learner is embedded in the public service philosophy of many librarians. Public librarians' wide experience of supporting DL students makes them an important stakeholder in any discussions of library provision for distance learners. As this report shows, public librarians are well placed to comment on the extent to which DL students have received adequate and appropriate training and guidance in library and information retrieval skills as part of their postgraduate course.

Public librarians would welcome more liaison with their colleagues in universities to help them develop their services for students and, where possible, to be kept informed of DL developments at local, regional and national levels.

Funding agencies and policy-makers should be alerted to the extent of the 'invisible subsidy' provided by public libraries to higher education and recognize the important role these libraries play in supporting advanced adult education and training. As a Central librarian in a London borough remarked:

> Public libraries cannot act as surrogates for their (DL students') parent institutions.

The following comment, from a Central librarian in South Wales, summarizes the complex interrelationship between the DL student, the host university and the public library:

> [DL students' needs are] the same as for anyone involved in formal/informal education—materials, study space, interlibrary loans, increasingly access to Internet. With the growing trend towards DL the demands on public libraries are increasing yet the funding goes to the academic institution involved, which in many cases does not provide adequate library support to students. It would be helpful if JANET was available to public libraries at an affordable cost.

CHAPTER 5

Course providers' perspectives on the role of the library in postgraduate distance learning

Introduction

It is clear from the data gathered for this chapter that practices and procedures are emerging as providers grapple with the complexities of delivering courses in the DL mode. Whilst the relationship between DL and libraries appears to have been a matter of concern and interest for many university librarians for some time, it is slowly coming to be seen as an important issue by course providers.

One of the assumptions questioned by this research is the notion of a DL culture which provides a unifying perspective capable of crossing disciplinary boundaries. Initial work on the project suggested that, on the contrary, it was disciplinary culture which might dominate people's perspectives on the role of libraries in DL. As the project has progressed, however, we can show that the differences between the way in which courses are designed and delivered do not, necessarily, reflect either the cultural norms of the discipline or the course providers' understanding of or adherence to any unifying conception of DL. The picture is far more complicated.

Because of its unique position, the Open University is the only institution which is named in this chapter. Course team chairpersons were interviewed in the following discipline areas: Arts; Technology; Education; and Social Science. At the time of writing, the OU course providers pointed out that the University's library at Milton Keynes was primarily intended to service OU academics and was, in reality, 'out of bounds' for OU students. This situation is, however, now being reviewed. In each OU regional office there is a member of staff whose role includes responsibility for library liaison. This may involve collecting and disseminating information about the policies of universities in the area regarding library access, and providing letters of introduction for individual students. The role does not, however, include negotiating access to libraries.

The course providers interviewed for this paper said they would welcome a national approach to library access by all universities. The OU has plans to develop electronic access to its library and is investigating how electronic communication will be integrated with print, but there are considerable copyright issues to be resolved.

Methodology

The chapter is largely based on a series of interviews with eleven course providers during the academic year 1994/95 and also draws upon additional course provider comments gathered via extended conversation by e-mail, telephone or post. The courses represented are as follows:

- Librarianship and Information Science
- Adult and Continuing Education
- Arts and Cultural Policy
- Teaching English to Speakers of Other Languages
- Environmental and Development Education
- Business Administration
- Management and Computing Science
- Dental Radiology
- Education and Special Needs Education
- Public Relations

Nine interviews were tape-recorded and detailed notes were taken during the remaining two interviews. Most of the interviews lasted for one hour, the shortest for 20 minutes and the longest for one and a half hours. The original intention was to conduct a series of semi-structured interviews with a representative range of course providers. For this we would have needed a comprehensive map of courses, but, to date, no such map exists and the situation is further complicated by the interpretation of the concept of 'distance'. When choosing a course, students tend to be more immediately concerned with 'flexibility' than with 'distance'. In the field of Education, emerging models of course delivery are blurring the boundaries even further to the extent that students who live less than ten miles from a university may choose to register for one of its DL courses, rather than attend a course delivered in the traditional face-to-face mode, because 'DL' provides them with the flexibility of study which they require. In addition, some courses, which do not provide students with standard DL packaged materials, still recruit students from throughout the UK as they are designed around a mix of short residential teaching schools and a programme of structured reading which students pursue using libraries nearer to their home or places of work.

Whilst there are some sources giving the number and type of courses on offer in universities in the UK, the rapid and largely *ad hoc* expansion of DL at postgraduate level means that such information is soon out of date. We decided, therefore, to select our sample of course providers in order to cover the following range of factors:

- those who had shown an explicit interest in the project;
- those who represented disparate disciplines, in order to allow for comparison;
- those who represented different types of course within the same discipline area;
- those who represented Education and Management (which cover the majority of postgraduate DL students);
- those who provided courses for librarians (as a potential source of good practice);
- those who stated their course does not require any use of library facilities;
- those whose courses were in the first year of delivery, for whom the identification of problems was still new.

Data gathering for this part of the research project was not confined to the actual interviews. From the first telephone conversations asking providers to take part in our student survey, 'off-the-cuff' comments have illuminated our perspective on this changing field and have provided leads and clues about how to conduct our research. At all stages, we stressed the consultative emphasis of the research and that the ultimate aim was to produce good practice guidelines for providers and librarians. Interview transcripts show providers beginning by giving information about their particular course and ending by entering into a dialogue about their perceptions of what was happening in other institutions. The pressing need for information about good practice, and for ideas in general to improve the design and delivery of DL courses, permeated all the interviews. To some extent, therefore, the project has already contributed to the dissemination of good practice and encouraged providers to contact each other.

We used an issues-led agenda to structure the interviews rather than devising a set of definite questions. This agenda reflects the key issues which have emerged as the project has progressed. By using this agenda rather than imposing a rigid template for the interviews, we believe we have encouraged our interviewees to articulate both their current concerns and their ideas for new developments. The interview agenda covered the following areas:

- *The course and the students*: questions posed to gather basic information about the structure of the course, number and type of students, nature of the course team, and so on.
- *The role of independent reading in the course*: questions posed as to whether the supplied learning materials were intended to be self-contained or whether students were required to make use of library facilities for all or any part of the course.
- *Access to libraries*: questions posed to ascertain whether any arrangements were made for students to gain access to the host library, to other libraries (e.g. via reciprocal arrangements), and the nature and scale of any difficulties encountered by students.
- *Training for library use*: questions posed to ascertain whether training was incorporated in the course, and the nature of such training.
- *Ideas for good practice and future developments*: questions posed to ascertain how far providers felt satisfied with current arrangements for library use by their students and the success or otherwise of any initiatives introduced to support students. Providers were encouraged to give their views about how local, regional and national policies and practices might be improved.

The following section summarizes the views of course providers taken from the interview transcripts and other recorded notes of telephone conversations, written communication and e-mail discussions. Data are presented under separate headings for each of the discipline areas chosen for the sample.

Management and Business Administration

For the purpose of reporting findings for this section, we have brought together two courses, which represent the discipline area of Management—Management and Computing Science, and Business Administration—as both serve similar student markets. Both courses reflect their discipline's tendency to see students as 'customers' and the need for course organization to respond to market forces. It should be noted, however, that whilst strong evidence of a consumerist ethos is present in both interviews, it is used in support of radically different course arrangements.

Institution A: Management, Computing Science and Statistics

Institution A is a 'new' university in England and has run a group of DL courses in this discipline area for 12 years. There are now some 500 students based in the UK, Hong Kong and Singapore. UK based students attend residentials varying from one weekend to two weeks per year and submit course work and a dissertation. The course director of one of the courses was interviewed.

Three linked comments illustrate this provider's belief in the need for students to make use of libraries and that it would be 'ridiculous' for courses at this level to be self-contained:

> It's made very clear to [the students] that this is not just following the notes game . . . We feel that if you're doing a postgraduate course you're going to have to do a bit of reading round . . . Students should to some extent be encouraged to explore other avenues of learning.

The extent to which students are expected to read independently of the supplied materials depends on two factors. The first relates to courses which require a high level of professional orientation:

> [T]he courses that we run are very much applied and professional in orientation, . . . very much into how you do it outside . . . so, examples, case studies—it's all that sort of thing they need . . . You can never put enough of all that sort of stuff in . . . I often get asked, why don't you put more examples in? And I say, well there are plenty of

books around which you can go to and look for further examples.

The second factor relates to courses such as Statistics, which have less emphasis on independent reading because they are largely 'quantitative or theoretical'. Even here, however, the course director believes that library use should still be encouraged. Making materials entirely self-sufficient is seen as both educationally undesirable and a practical impossibility.

Students are expected to buy books on indicative reading lists or obtain them from libraries, access to which is regarded as being the students' responsibility, regardless of where they live:

> I always tell the students that they will need two things. They will need access to a computer . . . and they will need library facilities. Now you can only say that. If they say, 'Yes, that's no problem', then that's it: you can't go into it . . . We give a qualification here, and they have to meet the requirements of that qualification. It doesn't differ if they live [nearby] or in Hong Kong . . . you can't lower the standard and alter the assessment requirements just because somebody lives somewhere else.

The course director is, however, aware that, due to the growth of DL and reducing resources in HE, students face difficulty in gaining access to other university libraries and that reciprocal arrangements are largely a thing of the past. He said:

> I think we were a bit slow in realizing this and the students have said, 'Look, can you set up something for us?'

As a result of pressure from students, the courses represented here are now trying to integrate the use of libraries much more closely with their general course organization; two key developments were cited:

- all students will automatically be registered with the library (previously it had been left up to students to register);
- a librarian attends the residentials to describe which services (including postal loans and literature searches) the library can offer.

Information technology was seen as offering only a partial solution to the problem of library access as many students are not in a position at work or home to make use of IT facilities. Some MBA courses do supply networked computers to students but this means increased fees at a time when students are under considerable financial pressures.

For this provider, universities need to appreciate the financial costs behind well-run DL courses and understand that it is not a 'cheap' way of increasing student numbers at a time when 'education is becoming more and more squeezed'.

Institution B: Business Administration

Institution B is an 'old' university in Scotland and the course in question, which operates in some 100 countries, has grown considerably over the last five years, as one of its co-administrators explained:

> It's hard for us to quantify exactly how many students we have because we don't have a timetable that they all follow. They work in their own time, so we have about 7,000 students on our database, but maybe only four or five thousand or so are active . . .

In direct contrast to the Management courses provided by Institution A, this provider takes the view that library use is irrelevant because the course is completely self-contained:

> [It is] a true DL course in the dictionary sense. We don't have faculty that we put out to students. We send them self-contained packs of information. They buy these packs and they do what they want with them. Hopefully, they try and learn from them . . . and when they've learned enough, they come back to us and say, 'Register me for an examination'.

The course is designed in this way in order to be applicable on a global scale:

> The crucial thing in this style of programme is that you cannot make any assumptions about what a typical student is, what his environment is like, what access he has to other students, tutors, and . . . libraries, so we make the

assumption that he has no access to anything other than the materials he buys from us.

As the course operates an open entry policy, it also makes no assumptions about a student's prior knowledge and is, in the words of the course administrator, a 'zero-based course':

Zero-based means that we cannot assume that any student coming up to the MBA knows anything about one of the subjects . . . so the author of the Finance course writes the course from the zero-based idea—introductory level right through to the final of the MBA.

The success or failure of the course is said to rest entirely with the materials themselves, which are produced in conjunction with a major publishing company:

[The authors] had a single overriding brief, and that was, 'You, the authors, are to blame if a capable student doesn't understand something . . . and that means they should not have to go beyond the authored material that we present them with'.

For the purposes of university statistics and to meet the needs of the publishers, students are surveyed but, to date, no information has been collected about their library use:

It's a question we've never asked of our students. That's why it's of interest to us to actually put [your questionnaire] out. Regularly we put out a fairly extensive questionnaire to all the students, it's about 18 pages long . . . the whole idea is to try and identify weak points or plus points in the programme so that we can act accordingly. But we don't ask about the sort of peripheral things like what other systems they use.

This is a course which makes a virtue out of non-communication with students and which sells itself on its ability to free students from having to have any interface with teachers or other means of learning support. Students do have access, via fax or letter, to an academic help-line but, according to the course administrator, this has only been used by a small proportion of students:

> [W]e've had a few hundred queries, out of a few thousand students, and when we analyzed these queries you tend to find that there's a core of a few tens of students who put in loads of requests . . . so the actual number of individuals who are not content with the self-contained and zero-based materials that we give them is remarkably small.

Education and related courses

Providers in four institutions were interviewed. Whilst library access and use were considered to be important by all the providers, the differences between their courses were as instructive as the similarities.

Institution C: Special Educational Needs

Institution C is an 'old' university in England and the course, which is mandatory for teachers working in a specialist field, has been running for 13 years, taking students from throughout the UK, Ireland and the Channel Islands. The director of the course contacted the project because she had already conducted a survey of her students regarding their use of libraries.

Although the course director acknowledged that the course aims to provide as much reading matter as possible by supplying core texts and copies of articles, she also stressed that students are definitely expected to supplement the course materials with their own reading:

> I've come to realize how important it is that students have the opportunity to go and use a library. That's one of the skills, they're learning to access materials.

Students are encouraged to draw on their professional background, including school libraries and any colleagues who have completed the course, for support in gaining access to relevant literature. Those students who work in Special Schools are seen to be at an advantage over teachers in mainstream schools as the former are far more likely to stock specialist journals and books. All students, however, are told at interview that, given that they are experienced professionals, it is up to them to find out where support is available:

> [T]hey're all qualified teachers, they're all postgraduate teachers. They've been in teaching for a minimum of two years, but usually about five years at least, and so they're all very committed . . . and so usually if they don't have access to the journals then they'll join the professional association and . . . start to receive the journals . . . Resources as a whole don't appear to be too much of a problem for them.

However, despite this emphasis on the expectation that post-graduate students will take responsibility for pursuing reading beyond that contained within the course materials, the course director acknowledged that, in reality, her students had very little spare time for this:

> [B]eing realistic, they're all working full time, they've all got homes and families to run. I think the amount of time they've got to develop these skills is limited . . . In practice it becomes a case of: 'I've got this assignment to do— right, I need to look for some background reading to fit in'. I think in reality they're not going to go off and search in the depth that we in theory might want them to . . . I think in theory they, too, would like to do more reading, but . . . the practicality of the situation is that they can't.

If students have problems getting hold of reading matter, the course tutors will only help in 'extreme' cases. This may mean a tutor will photocopy an article or lend a student a book, but each case is examined on its merits. Students are expected to support each other through networking and are allocated to regional groupings at residential weekends.

Paradoxically, despite the course team's belief that students should read outside the supplied materials, use of university libraries closer to students' homes is not actively encouraged as the host university is regarded as being, according to the course director, '*the* place for [the subject area] in my view in the country'. She did acknowledge that, as a DL student fifteen years ago, she had personally found public libraries to be useful, but only if she had ordered texts well in advance. She was unsure as to whether her own students would be able to get hold of the specialist books required for the course other than through their host university.

For this course director, IT was not seen as a viable solution to library problems:

> I found that so few people had access to the technology . . . I'm open-minded about it, but I think it's a long way off in real terms . . . I've never had a student in two years ask me for my e-mail number to contact me and I think that in itself speaks volumes. I mean people will phone and we encourage them to phone. We actually give them our work numbers and our home numbers and they will ring, but nobody's ever asked me for my e-mail number.

At one time, the department serviced a substantial course library but so many books went missing that this was abandoned. The department does, however, house the education collection from the university's main library and students are introduced to this at the first of their compulsory residential weekends. The senior librarian attached to the School of Education is responsible for the induction sessions and students are given some time for library work at further weekends, although this is difficult due to staffing problems and because library weekend opening hours are restricted.

The course director was uncertain about the extent to which students could seek help directly from the library or, indeed, about the exact nature of the relationship between postgraduate students and the library, despite the fact that she, herself, is registered for a higher degree:

> [A]s a registered student for a higher degree, I have been given a photocopying card. I haven't had to pay for it, I've been given it so I can use it in the library to photocopy a certain amount of material for myself. Now what actual transaction takes place I'm not sure, so it might be that these DL students have the equivalent, that they don't have to pay for these articles—that's the equivalent of their photocopying card. But I know students have said to me that the library has been very helpful in sending them information.

Whilst knowledge of the relationship between individual students and the library appears to be somewhat vague, at the level of course planning steps have been taken to develop much closer liaison between the library and course teams so that the librarian can establish the resource implications posed by new courses.

Institution D: Teaching English to Speakers of Other Languages

Institution D is an 'old' university in Scotland. This new course, which is expanding to Oman, Malaysia and the Czech Republic, has only a small number of UK resident students. There are no compulsory residential periods but the course runs in parallel with a full-time residential course and students can move between the two programmes, enabling DL students, if they choose, to have some face-to-face teaching.

The course consists of ten modules and a dissertation. The course team considers the modular part of the course to be self-contained as students are required to purchase prescribed reading:

> [W]e prescribe approximately five, six or eight books that we expect people to buy [for each module] and then we provide a resource file of extracts from journals and books. These two things combined cover all their reading needs as far as the modules are concerned.

There is, however, an assumption that those students who can use libraries will do so:

> I think certainly the students who do have access to a library are at a certain advantage to those who don't. I think what is good practice is for us to provide a minimum so that people are not positively disadvantaged, but I mean it's a reality of life that there are libraries and people do use them for purposes of study. I think it would be regrettable to treat DL as a special case and not a mode of learning.

As the course is new, students have not reached dissertation stage yet, but when they do they will be expected to make use of libraries. Even so, no formal provision has as yet been made to provide students with training in the use of libraries:

> I think as we move up towards the extended study, we will actively encourage students to seek the sources of funding that will enable them to come here for a month, six weeks, with the express purpose of accessing material and receiving supervision for the extended study, but I think that's highly dependent on finance. We can't really impose that. We took the decision from the beginning not to have a residence requirement.

To overcome feelings of isolation among overseas students, the course team hopes to foster self-help groups in remote areas and is looking at the possibility of employing local tutors and reciprocal arrangements with local libraries. The potential of information technology was being considered but was seen as very limited because of student demand and circumstances.

The course application form does ask students about their access to libraries, and is then passed on to the student's nominated programme adviser, although such access is not a condition of course entry:

> [I]t's really for our information at this point, trying to build up a profile of the average user of the programme, if there is such a person, and then their needs or strengths or weaknesses.

Students in the UK have normal user rights with the university library, but there are no specialist services for DL students. The course team is considering developing arrangements with university libraries and British Council centres in Malaysia to provide facilities for students if the numbers in that country continue to grow.

Institution E: Adult Continuing Education

Institution E is an 'old' university in England. This course, one of three which have been running for seven years, currently has 60 students working in post-compulsory education and training settings, all of whom have to have had two years' professional experience before beginning the course.

The DL course is also offered in traditional face-to-face mode and so the course team has been able to compare student experience across the two courses. For example, the students who work at a distance appear to be more independent and achieve more distinctions at the dissertation stage.

There is considerable emphasis in the DL materials, which are supplied to the students in the form of modules authored by the course team, on the concept of the 'reflective practitioner' and on personal experience. Each module requires the student to read beyond the supplied materials, and indicative, rather than core, reading lists are provided. As many students struggle to pay their course fees, they are not expected to have to buy core texts. Photocopied material is not supplied with the modules as the course director believes that this would amount to 'giving that material an authority over all the other things you could read, which we might not want to give it'. She added:

> We are more concerned with how the student relates their reading to experience and practice . . . Students get very hung up on finding the texts on our lists but we tell them to look and see what is available rather than worry if they can't get a particular thing. We like them to see what is available on the shelf—to follow their nose.

All students are expected to register with the main university library, which they can use if they attend any of the voluntary day schools related to the course or if they make a special visit. Some students have, however, complained about their treatment by counter staff and about the way in which their telephone calls have been handled by librarians. An additional resource for students is the departmental library which has grown considerably to support the DL courses and houses dissertations which students can consult. The librarian in charge tries to accommodate student need by being as flexible as possible over book loans, accepting books returned by post, photocopying articles, and carrying out literature searches. All these services are, however, offered on a somewhat informal basis as to advertise them would increase demand above the level that staff can currently manage. This library is used extensively during the course day schools and, according to the course director, 'students feel safer here than in the main (university) library'. The course team would like to see these services extended and also offered by the main university library.

The course team would like to develop e-mail networking, but a recent survey of students on the course revealed that very few had access to the necessary technology.

Institution F: Educational Studies

Institution F is a 'new' university in a relatively sparsely populated region of England. The Education department's potential student body is geographically dispersed and there is a lack of provision for similar study at other institutions in the region. Accordingly, the department has, amongst other initiatives, developed arrangements for students to study at off-site centres closer to their homes or workplaces. The department does not describe the off-site courses referred to here as DL, but recognizes that its students face problems of library access similar to those of DL students. The department has some 250 students registered for modules which can be taken on their own or, together with a dissertation, can be combined to make a Master's Degree.

This interview took the form of a group discussion between two academics and a librarian in which they considered general issues about the role of libraries and the need for liaison between academics and librarians. It began with a recognition that all part-time students faced problems with library access:

> [O]ur students are turning up on a Wednesday night, for example, for three hours of lecture or workshop and at the end of those three hours they go home . . . they don't typically have the opportunity to be near this site in the days intervening and, because they are practising teachers, they don't have much time, so a lot of the characteristics of the people being taught off-site apply to them. They do have a weekly visit to the site, but that is all . . . Free time to use libraries is at a greater premium for them and it's quite tricky to manage for them.

> There is not a vast difference in the student experience in terms of access to the library . . . If you do arrive from the staff meeting at school at 5.20 pm and you're taught through till 8.30 pm and the library finishes at 9 pm . . .

Despite these problems, however, students are expected to engage in independent reading beyond the supplied course material, for, as one academic pointed out, 'The assessment criteria require that people demonstrate a grasp of the broader body of knowledge representing the field'. And, as these criteria apply to all modules, independent reading should go on throughout the course.

The university library offers the same services to all students, regardless of where they live or their mode of study. For the librarian, the real problem for off-site students was the amount of time they have to come to the library:

> [I]f you come to the library during the day time, at any one time something like 80 per cent of the library staff are on duty . . . Come in on any evening and you've got two people . . . I don't disagree about the willingness. It's who you've got on and to what extent the students are made aware that if they want further [information] they can get it, and how they actually do that in your tiny little slot. All students have a need to learn how to use the library effectively, and what needs to be supplied is a combination of motivation, support and access.

To assist students, the academics and librarians have worked together on two initiatives. Firstly, academics and librarians have attempted to teach 'in tandem', as this academic described:

> So [the students] have a tutorial with me then are passed immediately across five feet of desk space to [the librarian] who deals with the information side of things. Our initial feeling about this is that it's a very potent relationship and one which actually encourages students to think about their needs.

Secondly, an 'open learning' pack has been developed to introduce students to the library, and this is given to students as and when they need it. The librarian, however, stressed that library induction should take place in the library itself (on-site rather than off-site), to encourage students physically to enter the library and meet the librarians, rather than rely on students working from information sheets:

How effective is it, for example, if I send them a sheet out—'this is how you use the catalogue', 'this is a strategy for your literature search'. How do I know that it's working or not?

The librarian also stressed the importance of developing students' skills rather than simply responding to their requests for help:

With telephone enquiries . . . I always try to make sure that there's some sort of development in the students at the same time. So I won't just do a search for them if I'm not clear they can't do it for themselves.

Although the university has reciprocal arrangements with libraries in neighbouring further education and HE colleges, the problem is that few have designated education collections. Online catalogues are being developed to link the university with its associate colleges.

The electronic library was thought to have potential, but also drawbacks, given the nature of the courses run by the department:

[F]or teacher training, in some cases, non-physical access libraries, I feel, are going to be undesirable—for students dealing with children's literature, and also the wide range of teaching schemes . . . where it's not so much the information you've got to look at but the material itself (e.g. pop-up books). You've got to be immersed in all the material that's around.

Concern was expressed about the strain on resources if students registered with other universities were allowed to use this university's library other than for reference purposes. The interviewees felt particularly strongly about the position of Open University students who need to make use of other HE libraries:

[A]lthough [OU] teaching materials are of a very high quality, they are not self-sufficient, and the students are required to read beyond the course materials that the OU provides. Where do they get this [additional reading] from?

The OU is now, to use colourful language, intruding into areas which were until recently exclusive domains of other traditional organizations like us. So they are sticking their feet into teacher education, which has been our business—our bread and butter, if you like. So we now inevitably have to take a view of them as competitors, rather than partners. It was easy in the past to say, 'Well maybe they are actually meeting a need for which we are not geared up—to the greater good and for the common weal, and all that sort of thing'.

But now they're pinching our business.

One of the academics suggested that a market philosophy for library services could be introduced, just as, to some extent, it already applied in the course, in the sense that students were able to buy single modules from this department but could also buy them from elsewhere:

[A] very modern way of thinking about it would be that university libraries would separate from the universities altogether and become . . . like telephones, or the computer services, or a cleaning contract, or the security contract. And you would expect students from anywhere, and you'd advertise and say, 'What a great service we've got!'. . . and any student from anywhere would come and use your services.

This suggestion was, however, opposed by the following view:

[The arrangements] we have set up have come about because we work in the same place and we see each other as being part of the same institution and sharing concerns for the students. And it's easy really—we had this idea over a cup of coffee one morning. If [the librarian] was part of a completely different organization and I had to pay him to talk to him about an idea that I wanted to do, this wouldn't happen.

Whilst the interviewees felt they had a great deal to do to improve the support they offered to students, they had also made progress. For example, the education librarian is now involved in course construction and attends formal course committees. The academics felt the onus was on them rather than the library staff to develop procedures for good practice:

> I've never found the library staff here to be other than very responsive and receptive . . . but I'm negligent sometimes in getting things like booklists to the library. Without that they're ill-equipped to do their bit.

> From my own experience the academic staff tend to sit down and say this is what we want on the course, and then we talk to the librarians once the rough draft is there, and then we look at the library implications. What we don't do, and what I'd like us to do, is to change the way of thinking about the course from the very beginning, think about students accessing information, the different sort of demands it will make, and to what extent we can modify, further use and all the rest of it, existing library facilities. So we build the library, in its broadest sense as a resource, into the whole process of course design, rather than sort of tack it on afterwards.

The librarian's view, however, was that liaison was crucial:

> [T]here's not blame thrown one way or the other. I think it's very much the communication side of things, the ability to be able to sit down and say, 'Well I think we could have done this', or 'You could have done it that way'. Now it's still patchy, but it's difficult to pick out an area and say it's not improving.

Other courses

Institution G: Environmental and Development Studies

Institution G is a 'new' English University. There are 36 students enrolled in the first year of this new course which has been established with European and Third World development funding. The majority of the students are resident in the UK.

Students study eight modules which include supplementary reading and set books. As the course is in the process of being developed, the first intake of students paid a reduced fee and were given the set books free. The first module is regarded as preparatory and demands that students read a substantial amount of material, a factor which concerns both students and course tutors. The course director said:

> I think unit one is pretty crucial, I have to say, but obviously you can't make people read things, and if people are under tremendous pressure, which they often are, then inevitably they tend to look at what the course work options are and work back from that. After this first time around the unit one writers are doing a revision of this, so that we actually decrease the size . . .

> [I]t is highly experimental and, considering that, it's amazing it's worked as well as it has. We've done a lot of evaluations and by and large we get pretty good feedback. . . . but of course most of them complain about the amount of reading, which we're now addressing. . . . I think it's better to start with too much and cut than to start with a fairly constrained idea of what people need to know.

The course director stressed that the course was still in its developmental stage, and communication with students about the expected levels of readings was important:

> We've got this category called further reading that's peppered around in there, in the study guide in particular, and students are not quite sure of the status. So I think when we revise all the units we're going to call it something like optional reading, because some of the students are getting kind of paranoid if they've not read every single thing, and it's far better for the students to be selective than trying to read everything and getting totally confused, so that's been a bit of a problem.

The course encourages students to attend day schools in order to create 'student networks of support' and to help them gain a sense of belonging to the course. Currently the day schools do not provide time for students to visit the library, the view being that by the time they have attended from 10.00 am until 5.00 pm, 'they've had enough by then'. This acknowledgement of the pressures facing students has led the course director to the view that the course should provide all necessary reading material:

> [I]t seems to me that, in terms of our students, what we need to do is to make life as easy as possible for them so that they get their packs of materials.

The course director added, however, that the dissertation stage may present the course teams and students with problems.

Despite the underlying belief that the course should provide all reading materials, the course director has liaised with the institution's library to increase the academic stock related to the course subject area. This has proved problematic, as the course director explained:

> Now I don't know how common this is, you would know better than me, but last summer I sent details of all the materials that we'd got in the course documents to [the library] and said, 'Please can you get these', and I think I marked some as being really important . . . And as I understand it they were all ordered and came in quite quickly, but then getting them onto the shelves was another problem . . . Some months later they were still down in the bowels of the earth somewhere.

> Quite frankly, the library hasn't got a lot of the stuff we need . . . A lot of the materials we've acquired here have been donated by publishers, or we've bought in ourselves, and they go out with the unit writers who write the materials and then when they've finished with them they come back in and we catalogue them for our own system . . . I anticipate that this will be quite well used later on in the dissertation phase.

The difficulties associated with gaining access to a sufficiently subject-specific academic stock have led the course director to doubt whether reciprocal arrangements for students to visit libraries closer to their homes would have any benefit:

[T]here's a lot of materials that we've brought into the course which are not just present in the library. Now that's our fate, and a big problem with our course is going to be the students finding higher education institutions which have libraries which have these materials. If you're doing a course in English and you're looking at Dickens or something, it's comparatively easy to find a library which has the books . . . So I mean it's a bit of a nightmare.

Institution H: Arts and Cultural Policy in Europe

Institution H is a 'new' university in England. This course is aimed at experienced professionals who are expected to attend the university for several intensive teaching periods of one week at a time during which they cover a great deal of theoretical material. Some library time is scheduled for these visits but is limited as the timetable is so packed.

The DL materials are largely made up of extensive amounts of selected readings rather than the more standard structured package. This policy is, however, being reviewed due to expense in general, but notably that of copyright fees. It is likely that the amount of readings will be reduced, rather than the extra cost being passed on to the students who would find any increase in fees prohibitive. The course team acknowledges that any reduction in the amount of supplied reading will mean that students will have to make even greater use of libraries than they do now. This in turn will put further pressure on libraries 'at a time when [they] themselves are under considerable pressure'. A further problem for the course is its need to use multi-media materials, particularly those on video and audiotape, stocks of which tend to be poor in most libraries. The use of networked computers will be of major benefit to access the range of material associated with the course but, again, this poses financial problems for both students and the course providers.

Students have to conduct fieldwork, including carrying out interviews with key personnel and obtaining local policy documentation, in a European location, from which they produce a 10,000 word dissertation. They are expected to read independently as, according to the course director, 'If there is to be any creative or research element in the course, there must be some independent reading'. Student evaluations have shown that access to libraries is a key issue and it is repeatedly mentioned in their feedback about the course.

The university has a specialist library which is well-stocked for the course. In addition, there is a librarian with a particular interest in the subject area. She has been involved in course planning and provides displays and bibliographies for the residential periods. The library is open until late in the evening and provides telephone and postal services for part-time and DL students. All students are given training in the use of libraries through well-developed, non-subject specific, learning support packages.

There are reciprocal arrangements with other libraries in the same region and, despite financial pressures, informal arrangements exist with specialist libraries such as that housed by the Arts Council. Students are supplied with letters of personal introduction to libraries in other European countries.

The course director stressed the need for courses of this type to have financial support through external funding in order to provide the necessary materials to students and cover the staff costs of writing more structured packages. Given the relatively small specialist audience, competition from similar courses in the UK and the rest of Europe may mean that this course will only survive through collaboration with other providers.

Institution I: Dental Radiology

Institution I is an 'old' university in the South East of England. This four year course attracts small numbers of students, who must be qualified dental or medical practitioners, from the UK and overseas. It is run by the course director with a part-time secretary. The course director said:

> When I set it up, I thought that it would be for people who are interested in Dental Radiology working in those countries that would find it difficult to send somebody to the UK for one or two years full-time . . . and that it would fill a niche for, I suppose the developing world. In practice that doesn't seem to have happened . . . We've had somebody from Malta, somebody from Hong Kong, somebody from Ontario, somebody from Johannesburg, a couple working in the Services, one from Australia, one in the Royal Air Force, and I think they were seeing it as almost an experimental way to see how DL works for Masters degrees—was it applicable to service life? And a certain

number of ex-patriots, one was in the Cayman Islands. But the big surprise was the number of general dental practitioners. And I think what they were interested in was getting a Masters degree that can be put on a register, that can be done by part-time study, by DL, by not having to come full-time. And the thing that has really surprised and excited me is the age range—one in his sixties, very enthusiastic, couldn't stop him.

Students are expected to read beyond the course material:

> Yes, yes, very much so . . . and one is carrying—what can I call it?—the basic philosophy that underlies, underpins, the British University system at Masters level, that one is moving from purely didactic work to one where there's a little bit of, hopefully, original thought.

Despite this 'philosophy' and the expectation that students will take responsibility in their own locality for securing access to 'adequate' library facilities, the course director acknowledges that such facilities cannot be relied upon and, therefore, course materials are designed to be as self-contained as possible, certainly for the first year of the course. Additional materials are supplied at the annual two or three week residential schools. In the fourth year of the course, students are expected to produce research-based reports for which library use is deemed to be essential. It is at this stage, therefore, that they receive a formal induction to the university library. The UK-based students have a definite advantage over their overseas colleagues:

> [T]he British practitioners basically have no problem at all. There are, first of all, the postgraduate sector libraries, where the librarians are very helpful. It's what they are set up for, to help practitioners, if they are members. The British Dental Association has a superb dental library and that does searches, supplies them by post. They have to pay for it . . . but most of the British ones are members.

The course director tries to help overseas students on an individual basis by carrying out literature searches for them to use when they visit the UK and by sending photocopied material, but this service is not formally advertised otherwise the director feels he would be 'inundated' with requests.

The university's history and collegiate structure is seen as being an impediment to the development of library support for DL students, despite the fact that the university has offered reading lists and examination papers to people who wanted to gain external degrees for over one hundred years. The course director explained:

> [W]e're in the unusual position that this course is part of the external system of the university, which is separate from the college. Now the students are registered with the university, but not with the college. [The college] doesn't recognize them and doesn't take an interest in the course particularly. I have an arrangement with the librarian and I pay for the services she provides.

Institution J: Public Relations

Institution J is an 'old' university in Scotland. This course is run by a department which has other DL courses in Management and related fields. It is regarded as being a Social Science course with a strong emphasis on theory, critical analysis and independent thinking, skills which are seen as being of importance for the public relations professional. In all their work, students are expected to 'make arguments and cite and present evidence'.

Each component of the course is accompanied by a booklet and several set texts. It had previously been the practice to supply additional photocopied material but this has been stopped because of copyright costs. Reading beyond the supplied texts is considered to be essential, particularly for the dissertation element.

Students have to attend for short residential periods at which some guidance is given in the use of libraries but the course team acknowledged, 'We are still learning about training for library use'.

The university library does not supply any special services for DL students and has discussed charging them more to use the library, though this proposal was considered to be unfair as the library is funded for these students through the slice of fee income which comes to central services. Due to the general lack of library facilities where their students live, the course team encourages them to come to the university library to carry out the necessary research for their dissertations.

Overseas students were seen to have even more problems than their colleagues in the UK and this was sometimes reflected in the poorer quality of their dissertations. In order to try and overcome these problems, the course team tries to supply overseas students with most of the material they need, 'in order to ensure fairness and avoid disadvantage'.

Institution K: Librarianship and Information Science

Institution K is a college of an 'old' university in Wales. This course, and an undergraduate degree (BSc), is run at a distance for students throughout the UK, across Europe and in Hong Kong. All students work in libraries and must have access to library facilities. Their circumstances, however, differ greatly as some work in very small libraries (e.g. in schools), some in isolated rural communities, and some in libraries which have very restricted opening times. Some students, therefore, do not have access to the necessary source material or collections which they need to draw on for the course. In addition, not all students have the advantage of working for supportive employers who can play an important role in making sure they are given the time and resources to find the materials they need.

Students' workplaces also differ in terms of the quality of IT facilities available and a recent survey of students on the BSc course found that many did not have computers at work. The course team is, however, developing ways to give students electronic access to the college's own collection and is beginning to use e-mail to communicate with students.

The course prescribes set texts which students are asked to buy and some reading material is supplied, though the course team stressed that, due to copyright costs, this is limited by expense. Students are given a letter to take to the libraries nearest their home and this usually grants them access:

> [T]he library community is generally very cooperative as people think 'well, if I help them then they might help me one day'.

However, the course team is aware that, as the students numbers have grown, some are now finding it difficult to gain access, and that HE libraries will take an increasingly 'harsher view' about who they will let in and use their facilities. The college librarian reported that he was having to contact libraries in some areas to 'try and ease the path' for students but that even he could not overcome the regional restrictions which have been introduced.

Students attend the college for a compulsory residential period and this gives them access to the specialist collection held in the library. The course does not provide training in the use of libraries, though, given the nature of the course, it includes units on information retrieval. Awareness of the fact that some students have limited access to adequate library facilities has led the course team to reconsider the way in which it recommends texts. For example, long reading lists tended to be prescribed but now more thought is given to prioritizing certain texts. The course team members believe that they face a genuine dilemma in that, on the one hand, they see DL as a vehicle for widening access to courses, but, on the other hand, they fear that by tailoring their courses in order to accommodate students they may be in danger of lowering standards:

> I think we felt perhaps a little naively that [students] ought to have [or] find it easier to gain access. I think as we've revised and redesigned the modules we've perhaps narrowed the focus, we've perhaps focused more on certain key texts, even at Masters level, but we make no bones about the fact they should read widely, you know, and that if they're going to get the full benefit from the programme they should read way beyond the basic texts.

Wide reading is seen as crucial to the dissertation stage of the MSc and so compromises have to be made. For example, if a student who lived in Yorkshire proposed a project which required access to materials that were only available in the South of England, then that student would be persuaded to think again.

The problem of student access to libraries is regarded as being partly due to geography but also dependent on student motivation. A student who lives in Manchester, for example, ought to have easy access to a number of HE libraries, but if unwilling to make the necessary journey across the city then he or she will be as deprived of resources as a student who lives in deepest Lincolnshire or the Outer Hebrides.

While the MSc students are told that the college library is a 'last resort', the librarian has introduced a special service for the BSc students which is advertised in the course newsletter. The library has bought (using departmental moneys) three copies of the three or four core texts related to each of the 23 units in the course. The level of provision is 'pragmatic' as it is based on the amount of money available to buy the texts rather than on any estimate of likely demand. The library has found, however, that, due to the pattern of demand, it needed to adjust the collection in order to increase the numbers of texts which relate to the first few units of the course. Students, including those overseas, can request these and the library pays the cost of sending them out by post—when the student returns them, he or she pays the postage cost.

In 1994, the library distributed 112 parcels at an average cost of £3.50 to a small number of students, one of whom lives in Orkney and relies heavily on the service. Students can also request, by post, items from the main library collection, literature searches and photocopies of journal articles. The librarian acknowledged that the service was currently problematic as it was open-ended and did not restrict students to a certain number of parcels per year. In addition, the service is being run by junior staff whose time has not been costed, and yet attending to some student requests takes up considerable amounts of time. The service is being monitored prior to a decision about its future. Whilst the librarian feels that students who have paid their fees should be entitled to use the college library and be provided with a postal service, he was also concerned that increased demand would put too many pressures on resources.

Institution L: The Open University (OU)

Arts
At the time of the survey the Arts Faculty had between 80 and 100 students registered for its modular Masters degree, which was to be expanded in 1997 thereby increasing student numbers to several hundred. Over half the students are graduates of universities other than the OU and they come from a range of backgrounds, including teachers, lawyers and librarians.

Independent library use is regarded as 'absolutely essential' for completion of the course; one of whose core elements covers research methods, including the use of libraries. In the foundation module, students would be expected to meet their tutor at a library and complete an exercise which requires the student to participate in and understand 'scholarly conventions'. This library might be one to which the tutor or the student has access. Students must also use libraries for the dissertation component of the course.

In recognition of the problems which students face in gaining access to libraries and the perceived inadequacy of public library collections, the course includes training in the use of the Internet and, from 1995, has provided students with the necessary software for their PCs. The problem is, however, that much of the current course-related material on the Internet is of poor quality or corrupted (though corrupt texts can be used for comparative exercises). An increase in the availability of networked computers is seen as a positive development in the future and the course chair pointed out that there would great benefits financially to the OU through wider use of IT.

Education

The MA in Education can be completed successfully without recourse to reading material beyond that supplied for the course modules. Indeed, the students are sent so much material that some complain about the amount of reading required. The course includes an optional Research Methods module, which does not cover library use or information skills, and an optional dissertation module which can be completed using only the materials supplied.

Attendance at a short summer school is a requirement of some modules. These residential periods are based on university campuses whose libraries are open to OU students whilst they are resident. There can be sensitivity about the level of demand, particularly if it is seen that OU students are competing with the host university's own students for library facilities. Some training in library use is provided at summer school and collections of course texts and photocopied materials may be housed in the host library or in the summer school office.

The School of Education is introducing a taught Doctorate programme in 1997 which poses considerable questions about the amount of library use expected of students and how they will gain access to adequate facilities. The course team likened the reading component of this new programme to a bouquet of flowers, bound tightly at the base of the stems and fanning out as the blossoms develop towards the top. But the question remains: 'How far up the stems do you keep the flowers bound together?'.

Social Sciences

At the time of the survey the Social Sciences Faculty was developing Masters level courses, though none then existed. Generally, library use is not essential to obtain a first degree or diploma, although the course team regards any library experience as being valuable for students. There are certain modules (e.g. Family Studies) where library use is required, and this is supported by the local tutor who provides a tutorial in library access. The foundation module covers basic library skills and this is built on at the compulsory summer school.

For this course team, the introduction of postgraduate courses necessitates a discussion about what higher level study really means and whether, by not expecting students to use libraries, one controls and determines knowledge. There is a danger that DL, without a stipulation that students should read beyond the supplied materials, lends itself to a competence-based approach and becomes programmed learning. This potential narrowness may be exacerbated by the development of courses on CD-ROM and the Internet.

Librarians in the future were envisaged as being managers of multimedia learning resources.

Conclusions

A clear finding of this research is that a single DL culture, with a set of concepts and principles about how such learning should be organized in relation to library use, has not emerged. Ideas about the relationship between the library and the course differ between and within institutions and between courses. To some extent, the nature of the discipline will influence the way in which the role of the library is conceptualized. Thus, courses which require independent project work or a sustained critique of literature tend to expect that students will need access to a library. Within the picture painted by an individual course provider, however, there can be conflicting viewpoints. Often, the demands of the discipline for independent inquiry seem to vie both with issues of equity for less well situated students and with ideas about the market and what it will bear. There is a lack of coherence in the way course providers talk about this which seems to reflect the incoherence in the circumstances under which the student must study and the institutional arrangements to support that study. The most internally coherent view about library access came from a course which does not require its students to use libraries.

Among those course providers who do require library use, aware-ness of the problems for the student is patchy, and strategies to solve these problems are being developed 'on the hoof', often without any clear sense of the financial costs involved or human resource implica-tions. But it is not simply a case of ideas being developed to catch up with a changing educational scene. Even courses which have been running for some years seem to have failed to develop systematic solutions. The picture is complex and chaotic. Some coherence can be found by looking at threads of discourse which run between different course providers, and upon which they draw in different degrees. The data presented above show examples of four distinguishable ways of talking about DL, which sometimes appear in the explanations of the same provider:

- discourse of Access and Fairness;
- discourse of the Market;
- discourse of Academic Standards;
- discourse of Student Responsibility.

Within individual providers' commentaries, examples of more than one of these discourses can be found.

The majority of providers are as much in need of guidance as they are able to give it. Institutions with the largest numbers of students, or the longest experience of DL, are not necessarily the best sources of good practice. Even providers of the courses best served by their own libraries are surprisingly vague when asked to specify the details of that service. Indeed, some of the initiatives for new services have come from librarians rather than course providers. Those institutions with greater experience of 'non-traditional' students in general are likely to have developed better services for distance learners. In the main, initiatives have tended to be driven either by student demand or by notions of the student as a customer.

Course providers appear to be in living in hope that IT will provide the solution to their and their students' problems, yet there is a great deal of practical development using existing accessible and affordable technology which could be put in place now.

There is a pressing need for better liaison between librarians and course providers to ensure that they share their expertise in ways that are to the students' advantage.

Any consideration of the library needs of postgraduate DL students will need to take into account the varieties of programmes on offer.

Four possible modes of programme are identifiable: self-contained; expandable packages; off-site taught courses; and practice placement programmes.

Type A: self-contained

The features of this type are:

- Course materials are intended to be entirely self-contained; the need for library use would be considered a weakness in the learning materials by the course provider.
- There is no residential requirement.
- Students do not normally register with the library.
- Some students may reside outside the UK and are often UK nationals working abroad either in underdeveloped countries or in countries where access to academic libraries is severely restricted. Their situation is treated as a benchmark regarding what can be expected of all students.
- UK resident students are free to register with the library if they wish, but the library would not be ready to meet a large demand for a different type of service.

Type B: expandable packages

The features of this type are:

- Course materials may be entirely authored by the course team and include opportunities for structured interaction, or may also include set books, readers or files of relevant reading with a study guide.
- Such courses would recommend at least some additional reading.
- They differ in the degree to which, or the stages at which access to a library is needed. At a minimum, library use would be expected for a final dissertation or extended study. At a maximum, some independent reading might be expected for each part of the course.

Library support for these courses might include one or more of the following:

- access to host library during residentials or day schools;

- access to host library on an independent visit by student;
- postal delivery of books or requested photocopied material;
- telephone services;
- literature searching;
- training in library use;
- a departmental library or information unit;
- information and facilitation of reciprocal arrangements;
- access to professional/specialist libraries;
- reliance on student initiative;
- electronic access to catalogues and document delivery.

Type C: off-site taught courses

The features of this type are:

- The course is delivered at a location other than the main site.
- Library facilities where the course is delivered may vary from an extensive specialist site library to a box of books recommended for the course.

Type D: practice placement programmes

The features of this type are:

- Students spend a period of their course in a professional placement, during which time they are expected to complete coursework.
- Library facilities at the placement may vary from a substantial professional collection to a deposit collection of prescribed reading.

CHAPTER 6

Student diary study

Introduction

In this study 47 postgraduate DL students kept a diary of their library use for periods of between three and twelve months from January to December 1995. The students were following courses delivered by twelve universities across the UK in a range of subject areas. Between them, the diarists returned 830 records of library use.

The study confirms several of the findings from the questionnaire survey and dramatizes the battle with time, institutions and resources which many DL students face. The research suggests that the burden of arrangement for library provision is currently not being fully met by providing institutions.

In addition, the study illustrates the currently clandestine nature of DL students' library use, while confirming the value which students place on making personal visits to libraries in order to browse among real books on shelves.

Methodology

During the course of the student questionnaire survey we approached approximately 3,000 students, asking them initially if they might be willing to participate in a longitudinal study of library use which would involve them in keeping records of their visits, as well as other means of contacting libraries. We wrote a second time to those expressing interest, explaining more fully what would be involved. We explained that the study was intended to cover a twelve month period, but in view of the fact that some might not be able to make such a long term commitment, perhaps because their courses were near completion, we asked for an initial commitment of three months, to be renewed in three month blocks.

Those students who made firm offers to participate were sent a ring binder containing a single Personal Details sheet and a batch of Library Log sheets, which are reproduced in Appendix 5. The Personal Details sheet was intended to glean basic information about the sample, including sex, age, employment and amount of higher education and professional experience. Questions were also asked about training received in the use of libraries. Actual libraries used were identified for the purpose of the public library survey (see Chapter 4). The Library Log sheets were intended for completion after every occasion of library use, including telephone, postal and online contact, as well as personal visits. The nature of each contact was recorded along with open-ended comments by the student, which could run onto a continuation sheet if necessary.

Guidance was given regarding completion of the diary and the return of the completed sheets to us at three month intervals. In particular, diarists were encouraged to be as open-minded as possible regarding the material they included in their responses, and assurances were given regarding confidentiality. Towards the end of each three month period, participants were reminded about the return of the diary and invited to participate for a further three months.

A large number of the respondents to the questionnaire expressed interest in the diary study and, of these, 47 firmly agreed to participate and made diary returns to us for at least three months. Of these, 35 continued for six months, 22 for nine months, and nine completed diaries for a full year. Invitations to attend a consultative conference, reported in Chapter 7, were accepted by five of the diarists.

Characteristics of the sample

The sample for study was essentially drawn from volunteers. One must assume that the diarists are a self-selected group of enthusiasts for library use, invited from a sample of already self-selected questionnaire respondents. Any conclusions from the study must be read with this in mind. Table 24 represents the characteristics of the diary sample.

Training in library use varied from having never received any at all, to very extensive for a participant holding a senior position in an academic library. Table 25 shows the numbers indicating various aspects of previous training for current and previous courses.

Table 24: Characteristics of the diary sample

Subject:					
Education	Management	LIS	Law	Medical	
15	12	15	3	2	

Residence:				
Scotland	Wales	N.I.	England	
5	3	2	37	

Age:		
Youngest	Average	Oldest
26	39	51

Gender:	
Female	Male
30	17

Occupation:					
Unemployed	Teaching	Ed. Man.	Librarians	Medical	Other tech./ man.
1	13	2	9	5	15

Previous years HE:		
Least	Modal response	Greatest
0	3	10

Years professional experience:		
Least	Average	Greatest
4	15	30

Table 25: Training in library use

Training	Current Course	Previous Course(s)
received information pack	25	21
guided tour	15	28
talk by library staff	18	23
library task	4	9
hands-on database search	11	13
introduction to JANET	3	2
course unit or part of unit	3	8
Other	2	1

In all, six participants relied totally on previous experience in earlier courses, having received training in none of the above categories as part of the current course. A further 13 had received no training as part of the current course other than an information pack about the library.

The study was intended to be intensive rather than extensive, seeking information about the fine-texture of a small number of DL students' experiences with libraries over time, from which further hypotheses could be generated. In presenting the results, we do not attempt to quantify frequencies of particular experiences or views. However, in view of the fact that the profile of the sample in many respects reflects the 'typical' DL student as described in reports from the UK, Canada and Australia, some tentative generalizations may be justified.

Types and length of contact with libraries

Overall, 830 records of library use were returned over the twelve month period. For each record of library use, participants were asked to indicate the manner in which they had made contact with the library—whether by visiting in person, or through another person, telephoning, using the post, or making contact via a networked computer from home or work. They were also asked to indicate how much time had been spent in the process. Table 26 indicates how many times each of the above ways of contacting the library were reported.

Table 26: Means of contact with library

Contact	Number of times library used	% (of diary entries)
visiting in person	585	70.5
by telephone	142	17.1
by post	72	8.7
through another person	21	2.5
by online sessions	28	3.4
TOTAL*	848	

* This figure is greater than the number of diary returns because in some cases the same return was given more than one code.

The table shows that by far the most common way of making use of the library was by personal visits, which account for the vast majority of the diary records. The next most common mode of contact is by telephone, with postal and online contacts representing only a very small proportion of the records. The small number of records for online contact is interesting in view of the fact that 16 out of 47 of the diary group had access to a networked computer either at home or at work.

For 741 of the diary entries, a time was given for the period of use. Overall, the diarists recorded 666 hours and 25 minutes of library use. The average recorded length of use was approximately 54 minutes, with the longest record being 7 hours. Out of 563 personal visits, a total of 614 hours and 10 minutes was recorded, with an average time for personal visits of approximately 65 minutes. Table 27 gives times in minutes for all the recorded modes of contact. In each case the minimum time recorded was 5 minutes or less.

Table 27: Times in minutes for all recorded modes of contact

Contact	No. Records	%	Total Time	Average	Maximum
Personal visits	563	73.6	36,850	65.45	420
Telephone	136	17.8	1,745	12.80	180
Post	23	3.0	195	8.48	60
Another person	18	2.4	320	17.70	120
Online	25	3.3	995	39.80	180

Personal visits

Overwhelmingly, these students are making use of libraries by visiting them in person. A number of themes arise from the comments they make regarding these visits, which are described in detail at the end of this chapter.

Telephone contact

Use of the telephone was described for a variety of purposes, including enquiries about opening times, renewal of books on loan, requests for photocopies or books to be sent by post, and requests for literature searches. Comments ranged from the delighted to the frustrated:

This library is 25 miles away. I would have liked to visit in person and find out what other books were available. However, it was quicker and easier to simply renew books by phone.

[The librarian] is always so obliging and is able to answer queries. She always tries to get what you order and never appears to get tired of requests (she gets a lot from me).

Will supply issues (all four), [but] don't supply photocopies. Amazing. Must cost more to post journals.

So easy. Polite and helpful. No charge, despite being 12 days overdue.

Rang to discover if I could renew books by phone (the weather was threatening heavy snowfall). External borrowers must renew in person. Drove to xxxx to make a personal appearance and choose more books—a round trip of about 60 miles.

Want documents photocopying—phone answered and told to hold the line—five minutes later gave up as it was peak-time charges.

The lady who answered was very abrupt and told me she hadn't time to answer the phone and take details as she was busy—so ring next term when the students were back or better still call in next term and use the library myself. I was very angry . . .

Postal contact

Participants described use of the post both to receive books from, and return books to, libraries.

One of the books on adult education which I had borrowed was requested by another reader. The library sent me a note asking me to return it immediately, even though I had another week to go before I was due to return the book. I put the book in a jiffy bag and sent it back to the library.

Participants described great pleasure in receiving much wanted books by post:

At last. Just when I really needed it. I have until 20 July but I will be finished with it by then—great.

One participant described a postal service run by a local resource centre:

By using this resource I have been able to have access to a wider range of books and materials than I would have been able to afford to buy . . . The service is excellent with no charges and the books are usually delivered to your school and picked up one week later by the relevant member of the team who works in your part of the county.

However, problems were noted connected with the receipt of books by post.

[T]he book delivered was for last term's assignment. I feel I ought to read it to justify the cost.

Unfortunately, only one of the three books I received was really useful. Postal borrowing is an expensive way to browse.

None of this postal borrowing is cheap—I paid £3.80 today in postage in order to return material . . .

Visits by another person

Reliance on other people to gain access to books arose as a strategy by some of the respondents to the questionnaire survey. This phenomenon was also highlighted by Winter and Cameron (1983) for Australian DL students. Of our diarists, 15 made comments at one time or another which related to getting material through visits to libraries by other people. For example:

> My daughter is a student at xxxx and so she said she would look for a book for me. Unfortunately the library stock was very limited.

> Only open Mon–Fri, 9–5 during summer—not very useful for those who work. Have sympathy for my wife's enforced day trip.

Online access

Of the comments relating to online contact, the majority concerned the use of electronic mail. This confirms the finding of Ladner and Tillman (1991) that even for librarians, the most frequent use of networked computers is for electronic mail.

> E-mail to librarian re. library search she is conducting on my behalf.

> I now have e-mail on laptop at home so can communicate with librarian whenever the urge takes me.

> Sent list of six books/articles to house librarian via e-mail.

The following comments, all from the same person, concern difficulties in gaining online access for other purposes:

> Access gained to xxxx but couldn't get access to other libraries from there. Disappointing and time consuming and probably expensive. Will discuss with computer staff during summer school.

> I originally thought that I would be able to access various journal databases and do searches of contemporary material. However, so far it appears that although I can get into various library catalogues for books, I cannot get any journal databases. This is a large disappointment because it appears I'm going to have to continue to wear out shoe leather and beg physical access to local universities and pretend to be a real student so I can use CD-ROM services.

This is where I get frustrated. I don't think I know enough about the technology to make full use of it and the longer I'm using the connection the more concerned I become about the cost.

Use of the various types of library

Diarists were asked to indicate the library to which their comments related. Table 28 shows the number and percentage of comments relating to the various types of library used. Clearly, these diarists are making extensive use of libraries of universities other than those which deliver their courses. The second largest frequency concerns specialist libraries of various kinds. Frequently, these are libraries run by professional organizations or services.

Many of the comments regarding use of the various types of library echo those which were made in response to open-ended questions in the questionnaire survey.

Table 28: Types of library used

Library	Number	%
Host university	122	14.8
Other university	290	35.2
Specialist library	200	24.3
Public library	137	16.6
Further education	73	8.9
Other	2	0.2
Total	823	

Public libraries

While the diary group seemed to make proportionately less use of the public library service compared to the student questionnaire sample as a whole, nevertheless the public library seems frequently to be regarded as a good place to study and a valuable source of material, as the following comments reveal:

Used reference library for quiet study in preparation for exams.

This is a very small branch library, but it's always worth checking just in case. I did get one book which is relevant. Actually had all I requested, to my surprise.

No suitable finance or banking books—but OK for social sciences . . . I'm surprised by the number of suitable books a small public library . . . holds. It's also a pleasant place to work and the staff are generally helpful.

Did a couple of hours useful work to complete an assignment, but no books of any use to me available.

[H]as some gems but is really badly run. Signs are poor and are generally disorganized. Some of the books are quite good and there are a few people studying earnestly.

One diarist expressed her frustration with borrowing restrictions:

[D]ecided to see if the lending library was any good. Again, same OPAC and some of the titles I need are available. Looks more hopeful. Also did author search and found one or two not on my lists but potentially interesting and useful. Good. Joined up and proceeded to locate five books—three of them on my list. Then came the crunch—because I live and work outside the city boundary (only one and a quarter miles away) I can only have three books at a time. If I worked or lived in the city I could borrow twelve at a time. How phenomenally frustrating! The staff were generally pleasant but when I asked to see the Chief Librarian or someone with whom I could explain my needs . . . the shutters came down. Rules are rules, we can't make exceptions . . . why not try writing— all these and other equally frustrating remarks. Not the most relaxing way of spending several hours of a much needed three day half term, especially when I had hoped to get some serious reading done.

But apart from situations like this, several comments suggested a high regard for the public library service, and indicate the manner in which its use can be a family affair which is integrated with other aspects of life:

The library at the end of our road stays open until 7.00 pm every Tuesday. So, most Tuesday evenings after tea the whole family pops down. While the children browse through the books I look over the fiction and non-fiction, perhaps read one of the local papers, occasionally order a book from another (county) library.

This is probably off the point, but is [a] word in favour of my wonderful local library. I had reserved a book for my daughter's school work which was found to be out of print and difficult to obtain. In two weeks it was located for me . . . and was waiting for me to collect. This service was provided free of charge and with courtesy and a smile. If a little library can go to that effort for a six year old, I think it is an excellent service . . . I may follow up the possibility of them finding texts for me, as I walk past this library every day on my way home.

After a morning's shopping, nearly didn't make it to the library. However, I couldn't waste a holiday offer ticket by going home at one o'clock. Spent some time reading some sources in the Central Reference Library.

Host university library

While the host university library seems to have been used a little less than public libraries, several entries were made regarding its use during residential periods or special visits:

This was not wholly for the benefit of my course but as I was in xxxx for the study week of my course . . . I took advantage and ran several searches. Some were for work purposes, others were for things which I wanted to take further—having first studied them on the course.

This was during the residential weekend. A request had been made for the library to be open for longer than the two hours on the Saturday afternoon as on previous occasions—so we got three hours. I didn't find it easy to find the documents I had tried to request the previous day—in fact only two of the five as other people were wanting them as well. . . . Had to queue for a ticket to use the photocopier and then the queue for the photocopier was long so gave up and went in search of other material. I never used my ticket so wasted my money.

One student pointed out that the study school may not be the best time to select material:

I decided, given past experience, not to borrow any items. The idea of library time is to get some ideas for the second year project. I felt unable to do this, however, preferring to do some work on the modules before making a decision.

During the study school I really felt no pressing need to use the library—excellent though it is. It is not until I actually start working through the modules that I need library services.

Others commented on its timing:

Better late than never. Second summer school and only just orientated to library.

This session would have been more useful during first school as I had already found out how to use the service myself.

Another diarist selected a time to make a special visit:

After some discussion with my supervisor have decided to spend one whole week at a university library, preferably xxxx where my course is run from.

After then deciding to spend time at the library en bloc (the only way of carrying out a preliminary literature search) I then decided to commute for at least three days to xxxx.

Having made this decision, the same student experienced difficulties:

> I did not realize it was the end of term, the library is packed with students desperately trying to complete assignments. I couldn't get near a PC to carry out my search. (I should have thought about the timing of the visit. I had spoken to people at the university but no mention was made of difficulties accessing services at this time of the term.)

Another student described her frustration with limited stocks and high cost:

> I arrived at the library at about 1 pm on a Friday. I was not looking forward to my visit as from previous experiences I knew it would be busy. I would have to queue for the photocopier, it would be hot and stuffy, articles/books/ journals not on the shelf (frustration) and generally very tiring. And yes, this visit too lived down to my expectations. I started off with a search of the topic I was investigating, wrote down the names of the articles/ books/journals I would require—then attempted to find them. The university did not stock many of the journals or even law reports that I required. I knew this would mean that I either do not pursue those materials or go to another university library which of course is time consuming and expensive. I would mention cost here: I calculated that this visit cost me approx. £40 (train fare, photocopying £18, lunch, etc.)

Other obstacles to access were commented upon:

> Due to heavy traffic . . . I arrived at the library much later than expected. I wanted to spend about an hour there but I only had 15 minutes before it closed.

> Is the library now closed on Saturdays? This is not very helpful for DL students. The term might have finished but our work is continuous until October and has to be fitted in around full-time jobs. There seems to be an utter

disregard of our needs. Now I am going to have to pay
fines on the books as well.

One participant tried complaining of difficulties regarding loan
periods for DL students:

I was told this system is geared to the full-time students
and could not be changed. (So much for equality.)

One student referred to use of the host university library postal
service as follows:

Three pages of references sent to the library—a number of
them won't be in stock and all the articles requested are
fairly short. However, I reckon I will be very unpopular
(tough!).

In the absence of any postal service, one diarist asked:

[H]ow can a DL student use a specialized library which is
108 miles away from her home (two hours drive each
way) and only borrow books in person—yet have to complete assignments where one of the criteria for marking is
evidence of further research beyond the set books?

Other university libraries

Over one third of the records returned concerned visits to university
libraries other than the host library. These records confirm many of
the issues which arose from the questionnaire survey.

There can be problems getting legitimate access in the first place.
One student relied on her friend to get her inside a library which has
introduced restricted access:

My friend is studying at xxxx. They have introduced ID
cards so there is limited access, therefore she came along
to ensure I could use the library.

Another student described at length the problems she had in
renewing a reader's ticket and the response she received to a request
to extend borrowing rights:

I arrived today with the final book ready to discuss my case with the most senior person available if my card was still trapped. It was cleared as soon as the book went in. I asked about the date of expiry on my card and was told that it was up. The librarian offered to extend my card until August 1995, but once again warned me that the external readers' cards were 'under review'. I heard this phrase on the first day I received the card, which I believe was in June 1993. I questioned her further today about why this was continually under review and was told that the library's first priority was to their under and post-graduate students. If too many demands were made from outside sources the students would suffer and the library would be failing to meet their needs. I asked for both an extension to the number of books I could borrow at one time and the time for which I could keep them. There was no leeway on either. The levels had been agreed by the sub-librarians of each campus and were inflexible. I was also informed that many people were refused cards. Think yourself lucky . . . !

Limited loan periods can be a continual problem for these students. The following extracts from a series of diary records by the same student describe the problem:

Wanted to know if I could renew the popular loan book I have. If I could, then I would have taken it back to be renewed, if not, then I'd return it the next day when it was actually due. Wanted to know because I would be passing the library later on in day anyhow—thought I'd kill two birds with one stone. Receptionist couldn't tell me anything so decided to give it a miss.

Asked if I could check the popular loan book out again and, if so, how many times. Was told I couldn't really but was allowed to just now because it wasn't showing as being held and it's the holidays.

Wanted to renew book I was returning. Someone had put it on hold. Two other copies were being shown on screen but I was already late for an appointment by then so filled in a card to recall it.

Forgot I had to return a short loan book yesterday. Checked it out again and can hang on to it over the festive season. Unfortunately I'd already been down at university and was home when I remembered the book. A double journey—not so good.

Can take the book out until Monday. Can see I will have to work at the university some time next week instead of making double journeys just to renew this book.

Busy personal weekend means that I won't be able to work, therefore will have to do it during the week. Seriously consider buying the book I'm using from the reserve book room . . . it's such a drat returning it and checking it out every day.

Sometimes access to short loan collections is completely denied to the external reader, as is access to computerized databases:

Unfortunately as an external reader I was not allowed to use the computer index at all. This was quite galling as there were about twelve PCs and only two were ever in use during the time that I was there.

As with previous visits to this library, most of the books I would like to borrow are in the popular loan category and not allowed to external readers during term time. Makes you angry when some of them haven't been loaned for 12–18 months. Obviously the staff do not review these very often.

While problems with insufficient loan periods for normal stock books were mentioned, some people clearly experienced little difficulty in this area, relying on good relations with library staff:

Had a letter from the librarian at the weekend to say that my books were overdue . . . I almost always have my books overdue and take little notice of dates. The librarian also never seems to mind as long as he knows who you are and that you are reasonably responsible.

I went in to make my apologies and renew the books. This can be done over the phone but I always prefer to go in person and speak to the librarian as I feel it maintains a good relationship. I chatted about my work (which is a few weeks behind schedule at the present) and was on my way. The librarian knows me well enough by now and was not at all cross with me.

When students use libraries with which they are unfamiliar and for which they have received no induction, lack of awareness of services available may be a problem, generating a sense of personal inadequacy:

Sorry, I'm a slow learner of new systems!! Libraries should display cards/posters on what's on offer. This and other libraries leave it to the user [to find out about] possible services. A little more advertising please!

When students do get access to a nearby library, the stock available may not be appropriate to their course of study.

Not much of relevance—some useful periodical titles but most of the ones which are of interest have lapsed. More cutbacks, I suppose.

I had much better success than usual in the sense that five out of the eight books I was looking for were at xxxx. They obviously have more on research issues than xxxx.

Studying [this topic] creates some difficulties as it is a specialist area. Few libraries take the material needed for research.

My daughter is a student at xxxx and so she said she would look for a book for me. Unfortunately the library stock was very limited. There were a few books dealing with the broader aspects of the subject which she knew I'd already got or had access to, and little else.

Use of personal connections is a strategy used in order to get access:

> I visited the library with my wife who is a postgraduate student at xxxx. Many of the books I was unable to obtain from xxxx were available and using my wife's card I borrowed four books.

Several diarists noted the difficulty of using the library quickly when services are already overstretched:

> It's coming up to exam time and the library is really busy. All the terminals are in use everywhere—study tables/ booths are filled and the queues to check out books are long. Can't just dash in and out.

Opening hours are a continual problem, as is making wasted journeys, not expecting the library to be closed:

> Weekend opening is suspended during the student vacations. This isn't such a problem over Christmas when so much else is happening but can be at Easter. We still have units to work through. I prefer to use the library at weekends/in the evening, especially if I want to photocopy . . .

The following extracts show the frustration that can result from unexpected closure:

> The reserve book room was closed. Didn't read the notice properly because I was in disbelief, but had something on it about stock-control/taking. Of course the semester hasn't started yet but there are lots of postgraduates about. I will try again on Friday. I'm not making a special trip tomorrow just on the off-chance that they've finished doing what they were doing. If I hadn't walked away in disgust I would have read the notice properly and would know how long it would be closed.

> Read the notice properly today. 'The reserve book room is closed so that a stock check can be done.' The notice also

said that if you wanted a book you should ask at reader services.

This diarist couldn't help being angry at poor communication, despite professional sympathies and feeling guilty about lack of entitlement to access:

> Returned very angry. [The library] was being completely revamped. When I arrived, I found the system was down and there was no access to bookstock. I asked at the counter and the assistant was very pleasant and said that there had been notices up for some time warning about this. Unfortunately as I don't go that frequently I had no way of knowing. So a long journey specifically to get items to use over the vacation was semi-wasted. Why couldn't I have been warned of this when I rang earlier in the week? Fortunately I could do some photocopying, but when my card ran out, they refused to give me change. I know this is a policy (we do the same) but it was quiet, just before Christmas—what about a little goodwill? Too annoyed to complain (also that feeling of not really being entitled to access).

This final extracts sums up some of the issues and points to a possible solution:

> Quiet—vacation period—very pleasant. Read many articles and photocopied some. Re-read conclusions on masters thesis on xxxx. Had difficulties in obtaining it this time as external readers not allowed to book out theses for reference purposes in the library. Someone has been abusing the privilege. However, I was allowed to read it and left my library card at the desk—they knew I was a librarian. The whole question of facilities for distance learners needs looking into. Most DL postgraduate courses attract fairly hefty fees. Perhaps a proportion of this could be made available on a mutual agreement between student/university/designated library(ies) for full use and access by the distance student. Because I am (a) a librarian and (b) a former undergraduate of xxxx I have been allowed to use the library as an external user, free of

charge. However, privileges are being withdrawn from external users, e.g. thesis use, and in any case I have been informed that from October 1995, there will be a charge of £70. This I feel should be paid from the fees for the degree. In addition, most libraries charge external borrowers for online and ILL services, putting an extra financial burden on distance students. I obtain my ILL free from my own library but not all students are in this happy position.

Specialist libraries

Almost a quarter of the records returned concerned use of specialist libraries, including professional and workplace libraries. Limited though such collections may be, students seemed relieved to discover their potential, sometimes after frustrating experiences with university libraries:

> My organization (a social work training agency) has a small in-house library. There are now few recent books but there is a reasonable collection of reports, journals and newspapers. We also have a daily press cuttings service. Through the librarian I have access to the British Library Lending Service which is my lifeline!

The same diarist commented:

> I have never used work library before my course—now it is a place of refuge.

After several entries recording use of this library, she reported:

> Have just heard that as part of a cuts package required by government, the library is to be closed—probably at the end of March. From a selfish point of view I wonder how I am going to complete my degree. From a professional point of view I cannot believe that an organization with a statutory responsibility for education and training should be expected to manage without a library. Couldn't establish what is really going to happen. Is the library closing?

> Is the librarian to be transferred? What will happen to the
> British Library subscription? . . . I wonder how many
> libraries have suffered a similar fate in recent years.

Sometimes use of postgraduate medical centre libraries was
described:

> This library has excellent medical reference books. The
> library is building up its resources of other professional
> books and journals. It was primarily a postgraduate library
> for medics only, but since the library has been upgraded
> resources have been made available to expand the sources.
> The librarian is very helpful.

> I am using my workplace library due to extreme problems
> with gaining access elsewhere. After wasted days at [a
> university library] I found I was better off using my hos-
> pital library and relating my assignments to health related
> topics in a broad sense.

Other workplaces also have their resource centres which some have
found useful:

> I was on an internal banking course but had time to visit
> the resource centre which has a good range of manage-
> ment and banking books and journals. It is useful as books
> and journals can be borrowed for free and returned via the
> bank's internal mail system.

> This is one of the most helpful librarians and libraries I
> have come across . . . Really good service . . . Although
> small and pretty selective and restrictive in their choice of
> journals it feels good for a library of its size.

For those studying very specialized courses, a single professional
organization may supply services nationally:

> [This] is a very useful backup service as the local libraries
> haven't such a good range of librarianship material.

Even libraries themselves may have special staff collections. The following is a reaction to the decision to integrate such a collection into the main stock of a major library:

> Upset to learn that the staff library is to be integrated with the general stock collection and is no longer to have a separate area or identity. I feel that this is very much a retrograde step as it is so much easier to browse when all the material is housed together . . . Staff should be encouraged in the interests of continuing professional development to read professionally . . . it will certainly make my life that much harder when grabbing the odd opportunity between desk duties to search for key course books.

Emerging themes

While the above categories were imposed on the data prior to diary entries being made, in this section themes are described which emerged from a reading of the completed diaries. The comments are taken largely from the entries relating to personal visits, since this is by far the largest section of the data. However, the categories were also used to reclassify data relating to other modes of contact.

The value of browsing

A clear message from the diaries is that students value the opportunity to visit libraries in order to browse the shelves and keep up to date with journals.

> I returned all the books I borrowed and spent about an hour browsing through the school science bookshelves. Normally I would use the LIBERTAS computer index to search for books. In this case I was happy to just skim through books and choose the most appropriate.

> This library is 25 miles away. I would have liked to visit in person and find out what new books were now available.

> This is the reality of DL. As soon as assignments arrive I order books as they take time to arrive. I order books that

look interesting/relevant before reading the course material which means I might be wrong. I miss the chance to browse among library shelves.

Decided to have a quick scan along the shelves of my area of interest. Picked up two 1995 publications. It is exciting and stimulating to use a library which is purchasing books in one's area of study. I get great pleasure from my library visits. I only wish I could spend more time there. However, limited time has its advantages in making me think more methodically and more precisely about what exactly I am looking for. With more time I would get distracted and 'waste time' on all the things I see and think—'that looks interesting'.

Found browsing of journals quite fruitful and photocopied a number of articles for consultation later.

This is one of the problems of postal loans. One doesn't know how worthwhile a document is until it arrives. Titles are often misleading—more promising than the finished product.

Check subject index and browse shelves and find a few interesting and useful background documents. Great believer in browsing.

Browsed the shelves of the staff collection . . . and picked up a few books . . . that subsequently proved to be of limited value.

Eureka! It's amazing what you can find on the shelves if you really look.

Having discovered that a couple of titles I was mildly interested in were unlikely to be returned in time to be of use, went into Reference Library and found a 1995 book on shelves.

On the way back to the front desk I was just scanning the titles as I walked past and noticed a title with a key word in it for my next essay. I stopped and found two books which looked to be very suited to my needs. So much for all the referencing, cross-referencing, searching by title, author and subject. I left with three books—none of which I discovered on the databases. Am I using it inefficiently?

Just pottered through library related subjects and browsed shelving and catalogues getting rough ideas for dissertation topic.

It would be a delight to spend time during the day just browsing.

Spent some time just reading from current journals displayed, made some notes.

I really enjoy having time to sit between the shelves and flick through new material, but I do find I always get waylaid and start reading things which are completely irrelevant but interesting.

My last log sheet. I hope my contribution was of some use to your study. I never did step inside a library but I regularly visit bookshops—sometimes only to browse.

Library use as a clandestine activity

A distinctive feature of DL students' library use is that they operate around the margins of normal institutional services and practices. Library use does not, for most students, occupy its own protected space, but instead is run in parallel with whatever other life demands permit it, or is slotted into the spaces which are left after the demands of daily and work life are met, and after institutions have fulfilled their functions regarding normal students. This is evident from the questionnaire responses which indicate that some students do not consider themselves 'real students' and would like to be treated 'normally'.

From the diaries there is evidence that libraries are used in the nooks and crannies of space that are left between the demands of family and professional life.

At its best this jigsaw puzzle of demands results in an integrated picture of apparently harmonized reading opportunities. One diarist presented an account of visits to libraries in which professional demands, his children's development, his own personal reading and the demands of his course are all neatly dovetailed together:

> Tuesday is the only evening when the library is open after 5 pm. I occasionally accompany my boys who borrow reading books or research information required for home-work. I suppose I am encouraging them to follow in my footsteps.

> As usual, the whole family visited the library, which is about 100 metres from my home. Normally I browse through the books on the shelves or look through the microfiches. Today my son put out a search for any 'Dr Who' books in the region.

> I visited the college to observe a student taking my course. I went to the library to find out more about educational research techniques.

For others, however, conflicting pressures result in a less happy picture. One diarist put a car accident down to preoccupation with the course:

> Had a car accident on way home—very shocked—lesson to be learned—don't think about (the course) on approach to roundabout.

Another diarist seems to see herself as operating at the edges of legitimacy by taking her daughter to a university library:

> I had my twelve year old daughter with me who was going to do her homework while I carried out my own business. She felt uncomfortable as there were notices prohibiting school pupils from using the library as a study area. This was presumably due to lack of space but I was prepared to make a request for her to stay if we were challenged—we were not.

The experience of operating at the edges of what is acceptable is also evident in the following extract where borrowing books comes across in part as an act of theft, rather than a wholly legitimate affair:

> Now it is the school holidays. I had two little girls with me (the baby is in nursery full time so he is no problem). I sat them in a corner with some scrap paper, pens and scissors and told them to be as quiet as mice! In these circumstances, I have to find what looks promising as quickly as I can and then I can review it properly at home in my own time.

In the following two comments the pressure of other commitments, and the sense of using the library furtively, as if under cover of darkness, comes across!

> A very quick visit to the library en route to parents' evening—I would rather be in the library! Many of the visits to the library are quick ones in the evening after work. It would be a delight to spend time during the day just browsing.

> It felt grand to use the library in daylight hours rather than after work in the evening. It must be easier to be a 'day-time' student rather than fitting everything in after work.

The sense of illegality is again underlined in this comment:

> I seemed to spend a small fortune in photocopying charges, copying articles and book extracts. I noticed that a new notice had appeared on the copier warning people not to copy more than a few pages per book or article because of copyright, etc. I'm afraid with my very limited time it is a case of copy now, read later and whatever number of pages are necessary will be copied.

In the following comments library use comes across as pleasurably clandestine:

> Children went back to school today so I sneaked a little time off work to do an hour on my current assignment. I

could have done this at home or in my office but there is
something about library atmosphere which is settling and
enjoyable.

I found myself with an unexpected afternoon off and it is
the last day of school term so I indulged myself in simply
sitting and writing. I have always found the library a helpful place to write since being an undergraduate and
spending days in libraries. Today I did it with a sense of
indulgence and really enjoyed myself.

Professional librarians are sometimes able to run their study needs
and professional lives in parallel, although a lurking sense of guilt is
sometimes associated with this:

I work here now so spent a couple of hours in the library
finding out what they can offer me. This is great. Free
access to the Internet (from my desk) via SuperJANET.
Free ILL loans. Free access to BIDS. Free access to
OCLC First Search.

Have taken out 'illegally' a lot of reference material on
xxxx. Also a whole load of pamphlets from the growing
collection under the desk. Haven't exactly advertised this
but all the same they're on my ticket if anyone cares to
look—working here should have some minor perks.

Checking to see if my own libraries had any of the texts—
they did. I'm afraid I am guilty of issuing books to myself
for a year at a time (I honestly would return them if a user
reserved them).

While professional librarians might seem to be at a great advantage, one described that he pays for services just as other students
would:

This is one of the libraries I manage. I . . . pay the same
fee as our students. This is my home site library and also I
used to be the librarian here. I decided to pay for ILLs
mainly because I am aware of the real cost to the service.

Another describes the difficulty of telephoning for services from colleagues:

> Day off so ring work to check if they've got a couple of titles in stock in the Staff Library. To my utter chagrin phone answered by my boss, who sounded none too pleased at having to do such mundane task for a junior! If only one of the others had been around—just my luck.

A further librarian diarist complains that her own attempts to study incognito are interrupted by students:

> Microfiche reader in reference room—constant interruptions from students needing help using CD-ROM, etc.—recognizable as member of library staff (Saturday pm has only skeleton staffing).

Librarians are as susceptible to the feeling of operating in a grey area as are other students:

> A rare use of the enquiry desk. As a librarian I feel I should be able to work most things out for myself. Also I still have a guilty feeling that I'm not really supposed to be using the library. A more formal arrangement would assuage this guilt.

The pressure of time

As in the questionnaire survey, in the diaries time emerged as the single most pressing concern for these students. Almost 10 per cent of the diary entries made some reference to time constraints and this emerged as the most frequently mentioned theme. Diarists repeatedly complained about university library opening times:

> I was resident at the university 24–28 July in order to work on my dissertation. Horror! Only the Education library was open—others . . . were all closed for stock-taking.

> Library closed. A change of hours for a couple of weeks until the summer academic timetable begins in July.

Fortunately I had to go to the university on another matter so not too upset.

Several entries give a sense of general time pressure:

I hope to be able to catch up during the summer holidays, but work pays the bills so has first call on my time.

I was able to photocopy some of the articles I needed, but I simply ran out of time as I had to catch the train home.

Looked at two theses I ordered—not enough time. Have reserved them again.

Located suitable books but this time it was too late to borrow—it was 8 pm.

Three hours passed very quickly and I walked away with a fair heap of material. Unfortunately I felt rushed all the way through the visit and feel I could have benefited from a longer visit. However, with a full-time job and only a few days in London long visits to libraries are rarely possible.

No time (or energy) to do their other library which holds more useful material. At 8 pm on a winter's evening one loses enthusiasm!

Pressure of work meant that I hadn't completed my project therefore needed books longer.

[W]hen you also work, time is precious, and one resents being given conflicting information and being made to feel unreasonable . . . On the theme of time being precious—I don't do what I have told students to do in the past, i.e. don't just stick to reading lists. Virtually all last year, apart from project work, I stuck to what was on lists. Time has to be used carefully, and I never really felt up to spending time browsing the shelves—it was very much straight in and straight out. I don't know if this was partly due to the feeling that I was using the library under false pretences.

I could take another two and a half years to write the dissertation, but getting the degree this year improves the re-negotiation of my contract of employment, which is why I embarked on the course. I will still take two years after that to become chartered. I'm already 42—how old do I want to be when I'm finally qualified?

A distance learning student's day

The Follett Report (HEFCE, 1993) on university libraries offers an imagined electronic future in the form of a sketch of a day in the life of a university undergraduate. Briefly, 'Alice' is pictured working from her study bedroom and communicating with her tutors and the library via a networked computer, with access to a campus textbook server and electronic journals, which she pays by credit card to download. This is the nearest which the report comes to a treatment of the issues surrounding DL.

Below is an account of another fictional 'Alice', but one which is grounded in the current realities of DL. The story attempts to give a composite account of the experiences recorded in the diaries.

'Alice's Other Story'

Halfway through the course she discovered the need for a library. The course provided self-study materials along with a good deal of supplementary reading, but still there were points to clarify, and one or two things she would like to follow up out of personal interest. Already ideas were beginning to form for the dissertation, for which some wider reading would be necessary.

She hadn't much of a notion of what was available at the host university library. There had been vague talk at the introductory residential of registering with the library, but time had not been allocated for this and by the time they left she could see that the building was already closed.

She had a vague idea that the public library should be fulfilling some kind of a need here, and although she used her local library regularly for leisure reading, for the children and consulting *Which* reports, she was sure that the stock would have little to offer for the specialist nature of the course. Nevertheless she went to see what was available. The librarian on the enquiries desk was interested in her situation, having enrolled for a DL course herself. They found a useful basic text on the shelf, ordered a couple more references from the county library via the local computerized regional catalogue, and processed three interlibrary loans requests. It was difficult choosing the titles to order with her—thus far—limited knowledge of the field and not being able to browse. She was pleasantly surprised at how cheap it was, but held back before ordering another five titles for the next assignment. On the way back home, thinking about how long the librarian said it might take, she regretted this and hoped that the librarian would do as she had said and try to hurry things up in view of her situation. But she didn't really know how much influence the librarian would have on this, and wondered whether everyone could expect this special treatment.

At home, she decided to take a bit more initiative and give the local university a ring. She explained her situation fully to the person answering the phone, that she was studying at another university by DL, but got a rather unsympathetic hearing. The librarian said, 'We have enough on looking after our own students without catering for the semi-detached variety'. It felt like a major setback, but she decided not to give up and planned a visit to her old university, 25 miles away, but a lot nearer than the one running her present course.

It was nice to be in a familiar place, but she crept around rather guiltily, not sure if she had any right to be there. Last time she came here it had been rather a quiet place, and she remembered straining her eyes on the microfiche, and having to consult the card catalogue for references earlier than a certain date. Now students were queuing to use computer terminals which she supposed accessed the online catalogue, which she hadn't a clue how to use. It would be hard to spend a long time learning with that queue getting longer behind, and she didn't know if you needed some kind of password to get in.

She decided this time to chicken out on the catalogue and go straight to the shelves. She could have done with some direction in finding the right class numbers, but didn't like to ask for help in case she was asked to justify her presence. Browsing the shelves turned out to be more useful than she had expected. She didn't find any of the titles on her list, but found a later reference by one of the same authors, and spent a useful hour scanning some other related titles. She also found the current journals section and got side-tracked reading a completely unrelated article about something her daughter was studying. She considered photocopying it, but was put off by the queues and decided to leave it for another day. Whenever that might be. She had to go anyway, but made a mental note that the library closed at lunch time on a Saturday.

She went home excited by the experience and determined to give her next visit priority, perhaps even over reading the course materials.

It was another three months before she felt she could afford the time for another visit. This time she had a few hours owing at work, and decided to leave early in the afternoon and hope to make an evening of it. The traffic on the motorway was worse than usual and she arrived later than she had expected, about 4 o'clock. She was dismayed to see that the library closed at 5! Surely last time she had noted this as a day for late evening opening? Reading the notice with some care, she saw the words 'In term time' and the dates showing that this was still, astonishingly, the vacation.

She planned to at least make the best of the hour she had. But something had changed. The porter on the entrance desk had been replaced with an entry barrier with a sign reading 'Insert Card Here'. This she had not expected. Students were fumbling in bags for membership cards and gingerly passing through as if the barrier had only recently been installed. Her plans to make furtive use of the library were completely scotched. No option but to announce her presence and find out what the proper rules were for using the library.

She knocked at the door marked 'Private' adjacent to the barrier. She introduced herself a bit more carefully this time than she had when approaching the other place. She said she was a graduate of this university and understood that she could make use of it as a former student in order to pursue some research of her own. The response wasn't quite as warm as that at the public library, but she felt that the librarian was basically sympathetic, and rather apologetic that the rules were a bit tighter than they had once been. She gestured through the glass partition towards the queues at various points in the library and explained that an external reader's ticket could be offered at a reduced rate due to her former student status, but this would only allow borrowing a small number of books and for short periods. The short loan collection would be unavailable and interlibrary loans would have to be paid for 'at cost'.

It seemed like a lot of money, but she decided that this year's holiday fund could stand it. Once the forms were filled in and the cheque written, the library was about to close. This time she took a wad of information leaflets, including a guide to opening times and one about CD-ROMs available for student use. The librarian told her that a good time to come for a bit of peace and quiet was after the exams had started and before the summer courses began. There would be a window of a couple of weeks there, and it was still officially term time so the late evening opening would still stand.

When she made it the next time, it was like the library she remembered. No queues and somewhere to park your things while you went off to browse. She just sat for a while gathering her thoughts about the direction she would like to take in her dissertation.

First stop this time would be a database search. She had no experience of using computerized databases, but the subject librarian was happy enough to spend half an hour starting her off. It took her a further hour and a half to download and print something that looked like a respectable search. What if she had missed something? She wasn't confident that she had defined her terms well enough and knew that she would still have to rely on other ways of trailing the key material.

The search showed her the limitations of the library she had just paid to join. Hardly anything of relevance turned up in the OPAC. Her first reaction was to feel she had been cheated. Remembering her experience on the first visit, she went back to the shelves and found one or two relevant titles and a collection of papers by a relevant author which had not turned up in the search. From a quick flick through a periodical she had not heard of before, she found two papers that she could see were immediately relevant to her study. At least the journey was not wasted, but there was one key reference from the reading list, which was referred to in some of the material she had found, and which she knew she must read in order to see how present approaches to the field had come about. She knew now that the next stop would have to be her own university.

From home, she made one or two telephone calls and finally spoke to the subject librarian at her own university who was prepared to admit that, yes, DL students have a problem, and, yes, as a special concession to her she would personally photocopy a couple of references and send them, along with a key monograph, by post, as long as she was able to pay the return postage. She was sympathetic to the problems and was concerned about students sticking too closely to a narrow range of material.

The librarian also said that, with the expansion of courses like hers, the university was considering ways of improving services, but this would depend on additional staffing. Existing staff were pressed enough as it is. She looked forward to the day when DL students could search databases from home and make e-mail requests for material to be sent by post. She said that the university had an experimental project looking at just this.

Alice wondered whether this would increase the demand to come and look at books, rather than reduce it. She was beginning to think of her guilty and unannounced presence in her old university library more as the exercise of a freedom to browse. She was thinking of her own success in extending the boundaries of a reading list and a computer search by defining relevance for herself. She was beginning to remember that this was one of the things you were supposed to learn at university.

Conclusions

The age and experience profile of the diarists in this study seems to be fairly representative of DL students in general. A range of geographical areas and disciplines are represented. Despite a weighting towards library professionals and, no doubt, library enthusiasts, there is a characteristic gap regarding training in modern library resources.

The returns suggest that there remains a heavy weighting towards using libraries by making personal visits to them, despite forecasts of the imminent demise of the library as a physical place. The most frequently used library resource is the libraries of universities other than the host. Problems of access include entrance barriers, restricted external borrower status, limited loan periods, difficulty associated with short loan collections, unfamiliarity with local systems, lack of information about systems and practices, and absence of relevant stock. Better access is sometimes gained through personal connections, and concessions regarding the rules can sometimes be gained by keeping the librarian sweet through personal contact.

Specialist, including professional and workplace libraries, form the second most commonly used resource for this group. Despite sometimes limited collections, their use can be associated with a sense of relief after the battle for access to universities. The existence of such libraries is sometimes under threat from institutional reorganization.

For this group, public libraries were third in order of frequency of use. There is a commonly expressed view that the middle classes have abandoned the public library service in favour of buying books. This study provides some evidence for the esteem and affection in which the public library service is held by the adult learner. It seems to remain an important source of academic material, and for some its use is integrated with family activities, such as children's reading or shopping. The role of the public library service needs better recognition and support.

The host university library was less frequently used than the other three groups. Problems in the use of the host university library include both distance and inconvenient opening times when students do visit either for organized residential courses or by their own arrangement. Breakdown in communication regarding when facilities will be available sometimes occur, with libraries typically geared to the demands of the timetable of undergraduates.

Postal services are valued where they exist, although the cost and the waste involved in ordering material which turns out not to be useful or relevant can be seen as problems.

Getting information and things organized by telephone varies in success. The pleasure and relief at saving unnecessary and wasted journeys through use of the phone is mirrored by the extreme frustration experienced when the telephone response is unhelpful.

Several mentions were made of the use of networked computers in order to obtain library services. Where this group used such facilities it was most frequently for electronic mail. One student described the disappointment she felt at being unable to access databases through an Internet connection with her host university library.

The need to browse books on shelves came across strongly from these diaries. In addition to a concern with time pressure, which mirrors the findings of our questionnaire survey, this study has revealed a clandestine aspect to library use for DL students. The diaries suggest that library use for these students has an air of illegitimacy. Students see themselves as operating outside the normal expectations of academic and student life, and hanker after a legitimization of their study needs. It may be that this sense of illegitimacy can be partly alleviated through better communication and training.

Students want the opportunity to browse for extended periods before deciding what to take home and read in depth. Access to nearby libraries can be expensive and limited in the services which are offered. But even if these difficulties can be overcome, the stock of a local institution may not reflect the reading demands of a particular course. Despite this, extensive use is being made by this group of local university libraries, in excess of the use made of the host university library.

It seems that students would benefit from a library service which integrated some measure of local university access with some measure of special arrangements by the host institution, ensuring that access is available to the specialist material that a course may require. Formal arrangements are required to meet the needs of this growing body of students.

CHAPTER 7

Conclusions and recommendations

The research questions

The studies reported in this volume were designed, as the Introduction made clear, to provide answers to a number of related questions, namely:

- what are the experiences of students with regard to the use of libraries on postgraduate DL programmes in the UK?
- what arrangements are course providers making for library use?
- how do university librarians perceive the role of the university library in such programmes?
- in what ways and to what extent do public libraries support DL students?

We pointed out, also, that the study raised important questions as to how DL courses are aiding or hindering the development of independent learners through their library policies and we asked how developments in technology are impinging on the availability of library facilities. In this concluding chapter we shall summarize the evidence gained from our studies with these questions in mind, and then suggest what future research is needed and what recommendations for practice can be made.

Literature review

A review of the international literature revealed many common themes:

- Problems of library access are being inadequately addressed.

- There is concern in all areas that students are not making sufficient use even of those services that are available to them.
- Distance learning seems to represent a trend towards the exclusion of the library, against the background of librarians having already been inadequately involved in course and curriculum planning.
- In the UK, North America and Australia, the reliance of students on public library services emerges as an issue. Despite apparently relatively poor levels of provision, North American and Australian students make at least as extensive use of the public library service as they do of those of the parent institution.
- The profile of the type of student served by the recent expansion is the same across countries. Because students are mature and inexperienced in the use of modern library resources, they are in greater need of bibliographic instruction or user education than those students who have been traditionally served by university libraries.
- There is a significant lack of detailed elaborations of educational perspectives on the role of the library in distance learning, or attempts to map the course provider's view through research.

The findings of the present study confirm and amplify these concerns. It is clear that in the UK, as in the USA, Canada, and Australia, the significant recent expansion in the numbers of students on DL courses has not been matched with the implementation of measures that will effectively meet library needs.

The student experience

Of the 977 students who completed the questionnaire, 72 per cent reported using the library as part of their course.

A minority of students believe that DL courses should contain all necessary reading material. However, the majority view was that the use of a library is an essential aspect of study at this level.

Although the majority of students see great value in using libraries, they had also experienced many obstacles. Lack of training, an absence of basic information about their rights as students, lack of access to the services of their nearest university library (except normally for browsing) and a reliance upon the limited resources of the local public library, all contribute to an unsatisfactory state of affairs.

There is a clear preference, evident from both the questionnaire responses and the diary study, for better access to local university facilities. A frequently expressed view was that universities ought to coordinate their activities to provide reciprocal access. This absence is a matter of serious concern for a large number of students.

Students report using public libraries more frequently than their nearest university library or specialist library, with visits to host university libraries being significantly lower than all other types of library. However, despite recognition of the value of public libraries, a number of respondents indicated that their public library is inadequately resourced for their needs. Similarly, there is a view that the local university library perceives other universities' DL students as a low priority. Indeed, the diaries suggest that library use can take on an air of illegitimacy as students see themselves as operating outside the normal expectations of academic and student life.

Course provider arrangements

Whilst a small number of institutions have established special 'remote' services, such as postal loans and access to electronic literature searching, the majority of course providers do not recognize DL students as a category requiring special treatment. Judging from comments made by students, there is a need for improvement in such matters as training in library use and information about library access and borrowing rights. The overriding impression from our data is that many course providers are only superficially addressing the issue of their students' library needs.

Interviews with course providers reveal a lack of sustained and coherent thinking about how student learning should be organized in relation to library use. There are different views within institutions and few systematic, well articulated solutions.

Course providers tend not to involve their university librarian colleagues in the planning and delivery of courses.

The role of the university library

The vast majority of university libraries do not have a dedicated DL librarian and most do not distinguish between DL and other part-time students.

Special library services for DL students are offered by a high proportion of university libraries: telephone renewals (93.1 per cent);
literature searches (63.2 per cent); photocopying articles requested by
students (58.6 per cent); sending articles by post (68.4 per cent).
However, just under two-thirds do not provide a leaflet describing
such services, and there are very few examples of libraries which have
established postal services for all DL students and advertise these.

Sixty-three per cent of libraries report allowing DL students from
other institutions to use their facilities for reference purposes, while
28.7 per cent allow access under certain circumstances, and 8.3 per
cent do not allow access.

Several libraries report having reciprocal arrangements with others
for research students and academic staff only, but only in a small
number of cases did these arrangements extend to all students. The
picture is, however, very confused, with librarians expressing doubts
about the precise nature of the arrangements. It is clear from our data
that reciprocal arrangements only account for a minority of the provision for DL students. Moreover, while most librarians believe that
effective and fair reciprocal arrangements must be developed, many
problems are raised and there are fears that well-stocked libraries will
suffer, 'paying' in effect for the neglect of students by other libraries.

Many librarians refer to a lack of adequate liaison with academic
departments as a cause of frustration.

The majority of respondents refer to staffing and resource problems
as being the major obstacles to improving services.

The general picture that emerges from the responses of university
librarians is of an awareness of the somewhat *ad hoc* and unsatisfactory state of affairs currently prevailing, coupled with a willingness
and desire to secure more effective services for DL students.

The role of public libraries

The vast majority of public libraries do not distinguish students in
their user records, let alone DL students, but, despite an acknowledged inadequacy of resources for university study, the evidence
points to students making extensive use of public libraries. Public
librarians perceive their role as that of public service, supporting the
lifelong learning of adults, whether they are registered on courses or
not.

Public librarians feel they can play an important role by acting as a
'gateway' for students, directing them to relevant collections. Better

liaison with universities and access to IT facilities such as JANET would help considerably in the fulfilment of this role.

Our survey shows the important and largely hidden role played by public libraries in the lives of postgraduate DL students who make considerable use of public library services. The reductions in funding of these libraries can only be a matter of great concern for the academic community seeking to enlarge DL provision.

Resourcing independent learning

The majority of students in our sample believe that use of the library plays a central role in their learning, seeing the selection of further reading as an integral part of their professional development. DL courses are, for the most part, based upon a pedagogy that aims to foster critical inquiry and independent learning. Since independent learning depends crucially upon the availability of appropriate resources for searching and selection, the adequacy of library resources is likely to play a very significant role in the success or failure of courses to meet a major objective. The research reported in this volume has, we believe, many immediate practical implications, but it is also, arguably, of fundamental educational significance in allowing us to understand the actual, as well as the intended, realities of autonomous learning. Judged from this perspective, it must be said, our research data present a disturbing picture. Course providers, in general, do not clearly articulate a consistent and coherent use of the library, and often neglect to equip students with the means, whether information or training, of making effective use of libraries. Students experience a confusing diversity of provision which, with all the obstacles this presents, makes 'further reading' a more time-consuming and less effective procedure than it should be.

Our research also shows another reality, namely that the much publicized promise of technology revolutionizing information retrieval and modes of study remains a promise and has not been realized for the students in our sample. A minority of students do have access to the JANET network which provides valuable access to databases, abstracting services and document delivery, but such services do not figure prominently in the library activities of the students in this sample, who are more concerned with such matters as physical access to collections, borrowing rights, and interlibrary loans. No doubt, were this research to be repeated in, say, five years, there would be more evidence of the impact of information retrieval technology. The need to give any technologically-based library use a sound educational grounding will, however, remain; it cannot be taken for granted that advances in technology will necessarily assist distance learners or be compatible with the objective of developing independent and critical learners.

Conclusion

Clearly, much remains to be done, both in implementing improvements in library provision which will be of direct practical assistance to students, and in basic research which needs to explore, among other things, the ways in which learning processes and outcomes relate to forms of access to library services. We hope that the research we have reported in this volume will stimulate such developments.

Recommendations

In April 1996, we invited university and public librarians, course providers, DL students and representatives of relevant professional bodies to a conference in Sheffield in order to consider the implications of the research findings. Some 60 delegates attended. Discussions at the conference resulted in a number of recommendations and key issues which are summarized below under the headings of the various stakeholders in distance learning.

Distance learning students

1. Students require more training in the use of libraries and this could be facilitated through computer packages. Libraries may be able to share their resources and pool expertise in this area, and possibly produce an inter-university pack.

2. Students require up-to-date information about the range of resources available in libraries and should receive this information throughout their course. Some students would be helped if they could borrow PCs on short loan.

3. Ideally, students would have library vouchers to be used anywhere in the UK. Students have a right to know what they are being provided with as part of the fee structure for a course.

4. Extended opening hours are useful but experienced subject-specialist staff need to be on hand to support students.

5. Course providers could assist students with their library problems by sequencing and pacing assignments to allow more flexible access to popular texts.

6. Distance learning students should have representation on boards of study to give them a voice within the faculty so that their specific needs can be heard and addressed.

7. If course providers and librarians raise students' expectations by promising better and/or more flexible services, those promises must be kept.

8. Course providers should give as much guidance as possible to potential students about the amount of study time involved in the course, the amount of reading in addition to the supplied materials and the expected extra costs (e.g. for text books, interlibrary loans, photocopying, etc.) over and above the course fee.

9. Students vary in their experience of using HE libraries: some are non-graduates; some have no prior experience of library use; and some have poorly developed study skills. All students want to have personal contact with librarians.

10. The concept of the 'virtual library' may help in part but students also want to work and browse in 'real' libraries. Developing research skills and learning that research can lead into 'dead-ends' are important processes for all postgraduate students.

11. Students should not be used as 'guinea pigs' to break down barriers nor should they be left to organize reciprocal or other arrangements on their own. The 'host' university library should help students organize library support in their own localities.

12. Students need clear guidelines about the demarcation of responsibilities—for example, how much of a literature search should be undertaken by a librarian and how much by the student?

University librarians

1. The definition of a distance learning student can be vague and so such students can seem invisible. Host universities should have clearly stated policies about their commitment to DL students.

2. Distance learning sits within an increasingly market orientated HE context and faces resource and budget questions along with all other aspects of HE activity. Universities need to develop clear strategies for DL and ensure that academics understand the resourcing issues associated with DL. The whole HE sector should work towards a much more coherent and collaborative approach to DL—Vice-Chancellors could play an important role here. In individual institutions, senior managers must show a commitment to DL and ensure mechanisms are in place for delivering a well-resourced service. There is a danger that DL expansion is being driven by the need to increase fee income (particularly in the case of overseas expansion) rather than from a specific interest in flexible learning.

3. Some of the concerns of DL students are also shared by on-campus students and more research should be done to compare the two experiences. In addition, more information is needed about usage flows.

4. The course validation process should act as an important mechanism for asking questions about the extent to which DL courses have addressed the role of libraries and liaison with librarian colleagues.

5. Reciprocal arrangements must be clarified and reviewed although, at the same time, it must be recognized that they are not the only answer to the problems faced by DL students.

6. Employers of DL students should be surveyed to discover how much support they can offer through such mechanisms as corporate membership of specialist libraries, supplying networked PCs and generally assisting students as they try to access library facilities.

7. Liaison between librarians and course providers must be improved in a number of ways. For example: course providers should endeavour to keep librarians informed of any new DL course being planned and of the numbers of DL students recruited on to courses to allow for planning; librarians should be involved in course planning; librarians should be involved in training students in library and information skills at induction weekends and/or day schools. Course providers, themselves, may need some training in effective and up-to-date library use.

8. Provision of flexible, well-resourced library services could be used to market courses.

Public librarians

1. The explosion in flexible learning clashes with cuts in public library funding.

2. Public librarians almost feel they are 'sitting there paralyzed in front of the problem' but want to support all students.

3. Closer liaison between HE colleagues and public librarians is essential. For example, information about course reading lists would enable public librarians to offer alternative titles to students and help them locate texts.

4. Students should be encouraged to talk to librarians (whether in HE or public libraries) as soon as possible, preferably before they start their course, to establish the level of help they might need and the type of texts they will require. If students had better training in library use, public librarians would be able to offer more effective help.

5. Funding should be provided to give public libraries access to the Internet.

6. HE libraries should accept greater responsibility for supporting their students and acknowledge the role played by public libraries.

7. Lessons could be learned from other European countries which have fostered closer integration between HE libraries and public

libraries and from countries such as Holland where students have access to libraries throughout the country regardless of where they are registered for courses.

Course providers

1. Among the reasons for the use of libraries by distance learning students, the nature of postgraduate study and the need to access a range of literature were highlighted. The needs of students below this level may, however, be different and this issue should be explored.

2. Course providers should attempt to ensure equity, given the diverse circumstances in which students live and work.

3. Course providers have to be aware of the problems their students face. They cannot presume students have the same experience of HE as they did and they also have to be aware of the ways in which HE has changed since they were students.

4. All students, including undergraduates, need to develop more effective library and information retrieval skills and should receive training.

5. Part of the top-slicing from DL student fees should be put towards services for DL students.

6. The Standing Conference on National and University Libraries (SCONUL) should be encouraged to push for a fixed national fee for library services.

7. When designing courses, academics could relate course objectives, learning outcomes and assessment to use of literature and development of research skills.

8. Given that DL is still in a relatively emergent state, particularly at the postgraduate level, course providers need a multi-disciplinary forum for the sharing and development of good practice.

9. It was agreed that SCONUL should play a key role in carrying forward these recommendations.

References

Aguilar, W. and Kaskus, M. (1991) Introduction to volume on off-campus provision of library services. *Library Trends*, 39(4), pp. 367-374.

ALA (1931) Adult education and the library: books for the extension student. *American Library Association Bulletin*, 25, pp. 674-686.

Allen, G.G. (1982) The role of the library in higher education and the implications for the external mode of study: an Australian perspective. *Higher Education*, 11, pp. 531-542.

Allred, J. (1992) *Open for learning: open and flexible learning in public libraries: the baseline survey.* London: The Library Association.

Anwyl, J., Powles, M., and Patrick, K. (1987) *Who uses external studies? Who should? A study commissioned by the Standing Committee of External Studies, Commonwealth Tertiary Education Commission.* Melbourne, Australia: University of Melbourne Centre for the Study of Higher Education.

Ashby, R.F. (1969) The Open University—a librarian's view. *Library Association Record*, 71(11), pp. 326-327.

Brophy, P. (1992) Distant libraries: the support of higher education students who study off-campus. *Library Management*, 13(6), pp. 4-7.

Bundy, A. (1988) Home institutions' library services to external students, survey December 1986. Appendix to *Coordination of library services to external students*, edited by C. Crocker. Sydney, Australia: Library Association of Australia.

Burge, E. (1988) Beyond andragogy: some explorations for distance learning design. *Journal of Distance Education/Revue de l'ensiegnement à distance*, 3(1), Spring, pp. 5-25.

Burge, E. (1991) Relationships and responsibilities: libraries and distance educators working together. Opening keynote address for the

Off-Campus Library Services Conference, Albuquerque, New Mexico. In *The Fifth Off-Campus Library Service Conference Proceedings: Albuquerque, New Mexico, October 30-November 1*, Edited by C.J. Jacob. Mount Pleasant, MI: Central Michigan University Press.

Burge, E.J., Snow, J.E. and Howard, J.L. (1988) *Developing partnerships: an investigation of library-based relationships with students and educators participating in distance education in Northern Ontario.* Toronto: OISE.

Burge, E.J., Snow, J.E. and Howard, J.L.(1989) Distance education: concept and practice. *Canadian Library Journal*, 46, October, pp. 329-335.

Carty, J. (1991) *Library services for distance education students: adequacy of provision: The Open University, Australia and Canada.* Unpublished dissertation, Aberystwyth.

Coles, B.M. (1994) *The loneliness of the long distance learner.* Paper based as a presentation to the Medical Health & Welfare Group of the Library Association, Annual Conference, Manchester, UK.

Crocker, C. (1982) *Guidelines for library services to external students.* Sydney, Australia: Library Association of Australia.

Crocker, C. (1987) Library support for extramural education in Britain: a report based on a five month visit to Britain as the James Cook Bicentenary Scholar, 1984-85. *Working Papers in Distance Education*, No. 11. Deakin University: Australia.

Crocker, C. (1988a) Library service in distance education. *Unicorn*, 14(1), pp. 172-173.

Crocker, C. (1988b) Meeting the information needs of external students. *Australian Academic and Research Libraries*, 19(2), pp. 495-513.

Crocker, C. (1991) Off-campus library services in Australia. *Library Trends*, 39(4), Spring, pp. 495-509.

Crocker, C., Cameron, M. and Farish, S. (1987) *A national library card for external students? An investigation into a possible system of borrowing privileges for all external students at all tertiary libraries: final report.* Deakin University: Australia.

Dale, S. (1982) The three L's—libraries, literature and learning. *Teaching at a Distance*, 22, pp. 72-76.

Fisher, R.K. (1991) Off-campus library services in higher education in the United Kingdom. *Library Trends*, 39(4), pp. 479-494.

Fisher, R.K. and Bolton, R.P. (1989) Library services for extramural courses: the results of a survey, University of Birmingham, 1987. *Studies in the Education of Adults*, 21(1), pp. 57-64.

Flanders, C.L. (1956) Off-campus services of the University of Michigan Library. *College and Research Libraries*, March, pp. 160-168.

Goodall, D. (1994) Franchised courses: the university library perspective. *Education Libraries Journal*, 37(3), Winter, pp. 5-20.

Goodall, D. (1995) The impact of franchised HE courses on library and information services in FE colleges. *Journal of Further and Higher Education*, 19(3), Autumn, pp. 47-62.

Groark, J.J. (1974) *Utilization of library resources by students in selected non-residential degree programs: implications for educational administrators.* Washington, D.C. : US Government

Grosser, K. and Bagnell, G. (1989) External students and public libraries: the student perspectives. *The Australian Library Journal*, 38(4), pp.303-317.

Harris, M. (1989) External users of a university library. *Australian Academic and Research Libraries*, 20(4), pp. 219-227.

Harrold, A. (ed.) (1993) *Librarians in the United Kingdom and the Republic of Ireland.* London: The Library Association.

Haworth, D.E. (1982) Expectations of teaching staff concerning library use by external students. *Australian Academic and Research Libraries*, 13(3), pp. 153-160.

HEFCE (1993) *Joint Funding Councils' Libraries Review Group: report.* Bristol: Higher Education Funding Council for England.

HEFCE (1994) *Profiles of higher education institutions.* Bristol: Higher Education Funding Council for England.

Jacob, C.J. (1991) *The Fifth Off-Campus Library Service Conference Proceedings: Albuquerque, New Mexico, October 30-November 1.* Mount Pleasant, MI: Central Michigan University Press.

Jacob, C.J. (1993) *The Sixth Off-Campus Library Services Conference Proceedings: Kansas City, Missouri, October 6-8.* Mount Pleasant, MI: Central Michigan University Press.

Jacob, C.J. (1995) *The Seventh Off-Campus Library Services Conference Proceedings: San Diego, California, October 25-27.* Mount Pleasant, MI: Central Michigan University Press.

Jolly, J. (1995) Distance learning support: quality support for distance learning students (2). *ELG News: Newsletter of the Education Librarians Group of the Library Association*, Summer.

Kaskus, M. (1994) What library schools teach about library support to distant students: a survey. *The American Journal of Distance Education*, 8(1), pp. 20-35.

Kaskus, M. and Aguilar, W. (1988) Providing library support to off-campus programs. *College and Research Libraries*, 49(1), pp. 29-37.

Knowles, M.S. (1985) *Andragogy in action.* San Francisco: Jossey-Bass.

LaBrake-Harrison, L. (1991) Extended campus library services: guidelines or standards? *Library Trends*, 39(4), pp. 375-387.

Ladner, S.J. and Tillman, H.N. (1991) How special librarians really use the Internet. *Canadian Library Journal*, 49(3), pp. 211-215.

Latham, S., Slade, S. and Budnick C. (1991) *Library service for off-campus and distance education: an annotated bibliography.* Ottawa: Canadian Library Association.

Lessin, B.M. (1991) Library models for the delivery of support services to off-campus academic programs, *Library Trends*, 39(4), pp. 405-423.

Masterson, W.A.J. and Wilson, T.D. (1975) Home based students and libraries, *Libri*, 25, pp. 213-226.

Maticka, M. (1992) Libraries and their place in the higher education process. In *Australian tertiary libraries: issues for the 1990s*, edited by C. Steele. Library Challenge Series Number 3. Adelaide: Auslib Press.

Simpson, D.J. (1971) Books and the Open University. *Library Association Record*, 73(9), p. 168.

Simpson, D.J. (1973) The Open University and United Kingdom public libraries. *Library Association Record*, 75(8), pp. 173-175.

Slade, A. (1988) *The second Canadian off-campus library services survey*, 1988. University of Victoria, BC, Canada.

Slade, A. (1991) Distance education programs in Canada. *Library Trends*, Spring, pp. 454-478.

Slade, A. (1995a) Paper delivered to San Diego Conference. In *The Seventh Off-Campus Library Services Conference Proceedings: San Diego, California, October 25-27*, edited by C.J. Jacob. Mount Pleasant, MI: Central Michigan University Press.

Slade, A. (1995b) *Topics to be researched on library services for extended campus programs: summary of survey findings*. Association of College and Research Libraries, Extended Campus Library Services Research Committee, University of Victoria.

Slade, A. and Kaskus, M.A. (1996) *Library service for off-campus and distance education: second annotated bibliography*. Englewood, Colorado: Libraries Unlimited.

Slade, A. and Webb, B. (1985) *The Canadian off-campus library service survey, 1985*. University of Victoria Library, British Columbia.

Stasch, M. (1994) *A survey of information sources used by students involved in distance education*. M.L.S. thesis, San Jose State University.

Store, R. (1981) *Looking out from down under: a preliminary report of a survey of library services to external students in Australia and Overseas*. Townsville, Australia: Townsville College of Advanced Education.

Swift, B. (1981) *Studying as an Open University postgraduate: the students' perspective: a paper prepared for the Higher Degrees Committee of the Open University*. Open University internal paper. (SRD Paper no. 196).

Unwin, L. (1994) 'I'm a real student now': the importance of library access for distance learning students. *Education Libraries Journal*, 37(2), pp. 11-20.

Walker, A. and Ward, S. (1994) *Unpublished user survey report.* Sheffield Hallam University.

Ward, S. (1995) Library supports distance learning students. *Sheffield Hallam University Newsletter*, August.

Wilson, T.D. (1978) Learning at a distance and library use: Open University students and libraries. *Libri*, 28, pp. 270-282.

Winter, A. and Cameron, M. (1983) *External students and their libraries: an investigation into student needs for reference material, the sources they use and the effects of the external system in which they study.* Geelong: Deakin University.

Wynne, P.M. (1994) The delivery of library services to distant users: the BIBDEL project. *Library Technology News*, 15, November-December, pp. 1-4.

Wynne, P.M., Panayiotis, P. and O'Farrell, J. (1995a) *Access to campus library and information services by distant users: preliminary studies.* The first report from the BIBDEL project (Libraries without walls: the delivery of library services to distant users) funded by the Libraries Programme of the Commission of European Communities. CERLIM, University of Central Lancashire.

Wynne, P.M., Panayiotis, P. and O'Farrell, J. (1995b) *Access to campus library and information services by distant users.* The second report from the BIBDEL project. CERLIM, University of Central Lancashire.

APPENDIX 1

Analysis of Library Usage and Access to Information Technology in Distance Learning According to Answers to the Questionnaire 'The Role Of The Library In Distance Learning'

This is an abbreviated version of the statistical report prepared by Donna Roberts of the Statistical Services Unit, University of Sheffield. A full version of this report may be obtained from the Division of Education, University of Sheffield.

Objective

The main objective of this study was to identify the best predictors of 'library usage' and 'access to information technology' in distance learning. Library usage was determined to be whether or not a student had visited a library in the last 3 months; this was looked at separately for host university, nearest university, nearest public and specialist libraries. Access to information technology was determined to be whether or not a student had access to a computer, and a networked computer. Thus, in total, six separate outcome measures were considered for analysis. Data obtained on 977 observations were analyzed using the technique of logistic regression modelling in an attempt to predict these binary outcomes.

Study background and assessments

Background

The study was commissioned because there was concern over library use of postgraduate distance learning students. Data were collected retrospectively on 977 postgraduate distance learning students. The data are based on the questionnaire 'The Role of the Library in Distance Learning', where the areas covered are: characteristics of the respondent, course studied and length of study, expectations of library use, attitudes towards library use, length of journey to different types of libraries, actual use of libraries, usefulness of material, detailed information about facilities and services used, training received, and access to information technology.

Assessments

Approximately 129 variables per postgraduate distance learning student were gathered. These variables related to the questions from the questionnaire.

In order to reduce the data set to a more manageable size, the client's judgement was used to discard those variables that were considered to be either insignificant or inappropriate as predictors. With these dropped, and any missing values accounted for, there were 10 potential explanatory variables relating to 785 postgraduate distance learning students for 4 of the outcome variables, 784 students for the outcome variable PC and 700 students for the outcome variable NETPC. The full list of variables that were considered for analysis are as follows:

- *Outcomes*

    1. Have you visited your host university library within the last 3 months? (visited/not visited)

    2. Have you visited your nearest university library within the last 3 months? (visited/not visited)

    3. Have you visited your nearest public library within the last 3 months? (visited/not visited)

    4. Have you visited a specialist library within the last 3 months? (visited/not visited)

    5. Do you have access to a computer? (yes/no)

6. Do you have access to a computer which can communicate by modem and/or JANET or the Internet, with other computers? (yes/no)

- *Potential explanatory variables*

    a) Sex

    b) Age

    c) Subject of course (classified into certain groups)

    d) Is it a requirement of the course to make use of a library?

    e) Do you feel the need to supplement provided course material with additional reading?

    f) Have you as part of your course had any training in the use of libraries?

    g) For how many years have you been actively following the course?

    h) How far do you live from your host university library?

    i) How far do you live from your nearest university library?

    j) How far do you live from your nearest public library?

Methods

Univariate analysis

Summary statistics were produced for each variable. The arithmetic mean, standard deviation, minimum and maximum values were computed for the one continuous variable 'age', while frequency tables were computed for all categorical variables.

Multivariate analysis

The multivariate technique of logistic regression modelling was used in an attempt to predict library usage and access to information technology in distance learning by identifying explanatory variables that are useful in making this prediction.

The logistic regression model can be written as:

$$\log\left(\frac{\text{Prob(event)}}{\text{Prob(no event)}}\right) = \beta_0 + \beta_1 X_1 + \beta_2 X_2 + \dots + \beta_p X_p$$

where β_i are coefficients estimated from the data, X_i are the independent explanatory variables and 'event' is one of the six outcomes. To estimate the probability of an 'event' occurring, the above equation can be rearranged to give:

$$\text{Prob(event)} = \frac{1}{1 + e^{-Z}}$$

where Z is the linear combination

$$\beta_0 + \beta_1 X_1 + \beta_2 X_2 + \dots + \beta_p X_p.$$

In an attempt to identify the subset of explanatory variables that are the 'best' predictors of the outcome variable, the 'Forward Stepwise Selection' procedure was used. Starting with a model that contains only the constant (β_0), this procedure considers all 10 potential predictors in turn for inclusion in the model. The predictor that is most statistically significant is entered into the model. With this predictor in the model, all remaining potential predictors are again in turn considered for inclusion in the model. After each stage of this stepwise procedure all predictors that have been entered are examined to see if they satisfy a removal criterion; if any do then the one that is least statistically significant is removed from the model. If no predictor meets the removal criterion, the next eligible predictor is entered into the model. This procedure continues until no predictors meet the entry or removal criteria.

As with all statistical modelling techniques, the final model was assessed for goodness of fit using a variety of approaches.

Results

Results of univariate analysis

The results of the univariate analysis were submitted in a separate interim report.

Multivariate analysis

The results of the forward stepwise selection procedure revealed a number of statistically significant explanatory variables. The following explanatory variables were included for each model:

1) VISITHO1   host university library
A respondent would be more likely to have visited the host university library if:
- training in the use of libraries had been received
- the host university library was within 50 miles
- there was a need to supplement the course material with additional reading
- the respondent has spent more than 3 years on the course.

2) VISITNE1   nearest university library
A respondent would be more likely to have visited the nearest university library if:
- the course states the requirement to make use of libraries
- there was a need to supplement the course material with additional reading
- the nearest university library was within 50 miles.

3) VISITPU1   nearest public library
A respondent would be more likely to have visited the nearest public library if:
- the course states the requirement to make use of libraries
- there was a need to supplement the course material with additional reading.

4) VISITSP1   *specialist library*
A respondent would be more likely to have visited a specialist library
if:
- the course states the requirement to make use of libraries
- there was a need to supplement the course material with additional
  reading.

5) PC   *access to a PC*
A respondent would be more likely to have access to a PC if:
- their course is 'Management and Business' or 'Library and Information'.

6) NETPC   *access to a network system*
A respondent would be more likely to have access to a Network system if:
- their course is 'Library and Information'
- they are male.

Goodness of fit of the models

A number of techniques were used to assess whether or not the
derived models fitted the data.

Classification table
A classification table was produced for each outcome in order to
assess how well the model fits by comparing the predictions to the
observed outcomes. For each predicted group (yes/no) the table shows
only whether the estimated probability is greater or less than one-half.
The overall percentage suggests the models are generally a good fit.
However, looking at each group individually, in all but one of the
tables (NETPC), one group is predicted very well while the other
group is predicted rather badly.

Standardized residuals
The standardized residual is the residual divided by an estimate of its
standard deviation, where the residual is the difference between the
observed probability of the event and the predicted probability of the
event based on the model. The standardized residual is calculated as:

$$Z_i = \frac{\text{Residual}_i}{\sqrt{P_i(1 - P_i)}}$$

where P_i is the predicted value.

If the sample size is large, the standardized residuals should be approximately normally distributed, with a mean of 0 and a standard deviation of 1.

The standardized residuals were plotted against the case sequence numbers. If the assumption of normality were valid, the points should be evenly spread about the value 0 with approximately 66% within +/−1. In all cases, this assumption appears to be violated.

Normal probability plot
Another way of checking how well each model fits the data is to produce a normal probability plot of the deviances. The deviance is calculated as:

$$\sqrt{-2\log(\text{predicted probability for the observed group})}$$

and a negative sign is attached outside the square root if the event did not occur for that case. The deviance is approximately normally distributed; therefore on the normal probability plot the points should follow a diagonal line. On the plots produced for each model, the deviances do not appear to follow a diagonal line, confirming that the assumption of normally distributed deviances is violated.

Conclusion

The technique of logistic regression modelling revealed a number of statistically significant explanatory variables for each of the six binary outcome measures being considered. It would be unwise to make strong inferences from any of these models as the model assumptions are not properly satisfied, but there was a clear association between visits to the libraries and: the use of the library as a course require- ment, the need to supplement course material with additional reading and the convenience (within 50 miles or not) of the library. There was also a clear association between access to information technology and the subject area of the course.

APPENDIX 2

Student Questionnaire

Code No.

THE ROLE OF THE LIBRARY
IN DISTANCE LEARNING

a research project of the Flexible Learning Centre,
Division of Education, University of Sheffield,
funded by the British Library.

Tick appropriate boxes ✓

1. Subject of course: ....

2. Do you have an Undergraduate Degree?   *Yes* ☐   *No* ☐

3. Sex   *Male* ☐   *Female* ☐   Age ....
    Post code
    first three or four digits   ☐ ☐ ☐ ☐

4. For how many months have you been actively following the course?   ☐

5. Are you in paid employment?
    Yes ☐   *Full time* ☐ *Part-time* ☐
    No ☐

6. Do you have domestic responsibilities which make it difficult for you to get to a Library?
    Yes ☐   *No* ☐

7. Do you have any disability which makes it difficult for you to get to a Library?
    Yes ☐   *No* ☐

8. Is it a clearly stated requirement of your course that you make use of libraries?
    Yes ☐   *No* ☐   *Don't know* ☐

9. Do you feel the need to supplement provided course material with additional reading?
    not at all ☐   *very little* ☐   *some required* ☐   *quite a lot* ☐   *a great deal* ☐

10. Have you used any library facilities for your course?
    Yes ☐   *No* ☐

11. If yes, when did you begin using a library?...

    If no, do you expect to use a library in the future for your course?
    Yes ☐   *No* ☐   *Don't know* ☐

12. If you have not yet used a library, but expect to on your course in the future, roughly when do you
    expect to begin?...

13. Have you as part of your course had any training in the use of libraries?
    Yes ☐   *No* ☐   *Please give details*

    ....
    ....

14.　Do you have a copy of your <u>host</u> university library's information pack for new students?
(Host university = the university which runs your course).
Yes ☐　　No ☐

15.　Is there a special arrangement for you to use a university library near where you live?
Yes ☐　　No ☐　　Don't know ☐

16.　Do you know how to get access to a specialist subject librarian for your course of study?
Yes ☐　　No ☐　　Not sure ☐

17.　How far do you live from:　　　　*please estimate*

	Miles	Travelling time
your host university		
your nearest university library		
your nearest public library		
any other specialist libraries please name		

18.　Do you consider the journey to use these facilities to be a practical option for you?
tick relevant box

	Yes	No	Don't know
your host university library			
your nearest university library			
your nearest public library			
specialist libraries			

19.　Roughly how many times **within the last three months** have you visited the following for your course?

your host university library	
your nearest university library	
your nearest public library	
specialist libraries	

20.　How useful for your study is the reading matter in each of the following:

	not at all useful			extremely useful			
your host university	1	2	3	4	5	Don't Know ☐
your nearest university library	1	2	3	4	5	Don't Know ☐
your nearest public library	1	2	3	4	5	Don't Know ☐
any other specialist library please name	1	2	3	4	5	Don't Know ☐

21. If you have used any of these libraries, how do you feel you were treated as a distance learning student?

Host University

Other University

Public Library

Other

22. Tick as many of the following statements as you **agree** with:

The course fee should include all charges for library facilities	
I am prepared to pay more in course fees that include library charges	
It is reasonable to pay an extra fee for a library season ticket	
Any additional charges would seriously limit my studies	
I don't mind paying additional sums for specific services	

23. Please tick the relevant boxes below.

	I require	I have used	I would consider paying for	I have paid for
Browsing the shelves				
Reading facilities				
Borrowing				
Borrowing by post				
Photocopying				
Reservations				
Journal access				
Supply of photocopies of requested articles				
Unpublished theses				
Government publications				
Inter-library loans				
On-line catalogue				
CD-ROM databases				
Training for use of CD-ROM				
JANET (UK academic computer network)				
Training in the use of JANET				
Access to subject librarian				

24. Have charges ever put you off using library services?

Yes ☐　　No ☐　　please give details

. . . .

. . . .

25. Do you have access to a computer?

At home ☐   Yes ☐   No ☐

At work ☐   Yes ☐   No ☐

26. If you have access to a computer, can it communicate for example by modem and/or JANET or the internet, with other computers?

At home ☐   Yes ☐   No ☐   Don't know ☐

At work ☐   Yes ☐   No ☐   Don't know ☐

27. To link a PC to an internet you need a modem. Prices vary around £100. Would you consider it realistic to spend a similar sum in order to gain access to library catalogues and networked databases?

Yes ☐   No ☐   Not sure ☐

28. Tick which of the following statements **you agree with**:

I want access to a university library for the standard service it provides	
I want access to a university library so that I can study like any other student in HE	
I only want access to materials relevant to my course	
I want access to range a of books and materials to further my learning in general	
Access to a decent public library which can provide the range of services I require would do for me	
I prefer to buy the books and materials I need	
I lack confidence when it comes to using library services	
A distance learning course should include all the necessary reading materials	

29. Are there any specific areas of access to library provision in which you would have liked guidance at the beginning of your course?

Yes ☐   No ☐   Don't know ☐

Please give details

....

....

30. Please use this space for any additional comments you would like to make.

Thank you for your help
Please return this questionnaire to:-
The Library in Distance Learning Project, Flexible Learning Centre,
Division of Education, The Education Building, University of Sheffield, Sheffield S10 2JA

APPENDIX 3

University Library Questionnaire

THE ROLE OF THE LIBRARY IN DISTANCE LEARNING

a research project of the Flexible Learning Centre,
Division of Education, University of Sheffield
funded by the British Library

QUESTIONNAIRE FOR UNIVERSITY LIBRARIES

Please Note:
*If your university does not currently deliver any postgraduate courses
by distance learning, please proceed to sections **B** and **C** of the questionnaire.*

A. Involvement of the library in postgraduate distance learning courses
delivered by your university.

1. Please indicate to the best of your knowledge whether postgraduate distance learning courses
exist in each of the subject areas below: *(please tick relevant boxes)*

	Yes	No	Planned	Not Known
Clinical and Pre-Clinical Subjects	☐	☐	☐	☐
Subjects and Professions Allied to Medicine	☐	☐	☐	☐
Science	☐	☐	☐	☐
Engineering and Technology	☐	☐	☐	☐
Built Environment	☐	☐	☐	☐
Mathematical Sciences, IT and Computing	☐	☐	☐	☐
Business and Management	☐	☐	☐	☐
Social Sciences	☐	☐	☐	☐
Humanities	☐	☐	☐	☐
Art Design and Performing Arts	☐	☐	☐	☐
Education	☐	☐	☐	☐

2. Do all postgraduate distance learning students following courses delivered by your university normally register with the library? Yes ☐ No ☐

3. If yes, at what point in their courses does library registration take place?

4. If no, please give reasons why library registration might not take place.

5. In your membership records, do you distinguish between distance learning and other part-time students? Yes ☐ No ☐

6. How many postgraduate distance learning students are registered with the library?
   (*If you do not have exact records please estimate*) ....

7. Where your library funding reflects student numbers, are distance learning students funded on a per capita basis at the same rate as other part-time students? Yes ☐ No ☐

8. Does the library receive a lower level of funding for distance learning students than for other part-time students? Yes ☐ No ☐

9. Does the library receive any earmarked or ring-fenced central funding for distance learning students? Yes ☐ No ☐

10. Does the library receive any additional funds for the provision of experimental or additional services for distance learning students? Yes ☐ No ☐

11. Please comment on any funding arrangements which may be relevant to the provision of services for distance learning students.

12. Please indicate the nature of your library's involvement in postgraduate distance learning courses by ticking the appropriate boxes below.

Consultation regarding the resource implications of new distance learning courses	Yes ☐	No ☐
Planning new courses	Yes ☐	No ☐
Writing course modules	Yes ☐	No ☐
Initial induction to the library	Yes ☐	No ☐
Information skills training during the course	Yes ☐	No ☐
Literature searching for project/dissertation	Yes ☐	No ☐
Course evaluation	Yes ☐	No ☐
Research into distance learning	Yes ☐	No ☐
IT projects involving remote access	Yes ☐	No ☐
Handling copyright	Yes ☐	No ☐

13. Do you have a librarian with special responsibility for distance learning students? Yes ☐ No ☐

14. Is this his/her full-time responsibility? Yes ☐ No ☐

15. Other staffing for services to distance learning students

No. of full-time posts . . . .   No. of part-time posts . . . .

16. Please list any branch libraries, or departmental libraries in your institution, that you know of, which provide services for specific distance learning courses.

17. Please indicate which of the following services you offer to distance learning students:

A leaflet describing services to distance learning students	Yes ☐	No ☐
Telephone catalogue enquiries	Yes ☐	No ☐
Telephone renewals	Yes ☐	No ☐
Telephone reservations	Yes ☐	No ☐
24 hour answer phone	Yes ☐	No ☐
Freephone service	Yes ☐	No ☐
Response to fax	Yes ☐	No ☐
Response to email	Yes ☐	No ☐
Longer loan periods or renewals	Yes ☐	No ☐
Special collection of books	Yes ☐	No ☐
Literature searches requested from a distance	Yes ☐	No ☐
Sending searches on disc	Yes ☐	No ☐
Photocopying articles requested by students	Yes ☐	No ☐
Sending articles by post	Yes ☐	No ☐
Sending books by post within UK	Yes ☐	No ☐
Freepost return within UK	Yes ☐	No ☐
Sending books by post outside UK	Yes ☐	No ☐
Access to JANET from home computer	Yes ☐	No ☐

Other (Please describe)

18. Have any of the above services existed in the past but been discontinued?   Yes ☐   No ☐

19. If yes, please state which ones and indicate the main reasons for this

20. Are there any times when the library is opened especially for
distance learning students? (e.g. at residential weekends)   Yes ☐   No ☐

Please give details

21. Please comment on any staffing issues there may be for distance learning courses
(e.g. weekend opening)

22. Please describe any examples of innovative practice or interesting initiatives in your institution's
library provision for distance learning.

23. In your institution, what obstacles exist to the development of library services for
distance learning students?

B. Reciprocal arrangements and access by postgraduate distance learning students **from other universities**.

24. Can postgraduate distance learning students from other universities use your library for reference purposes without charge?

Yes, regardless of institution ☐   Yes, in some circumstances ☐   No ☐

25. Please describe the level of demand by students of other universities for use of your facilities.

None ☐   Negligible ☐   Manageable ☐   Greater than we can cope with ☐

26. Do you participate in the book purchasing arrangement which allows bona fide members of the public to use the library for reference purposes without charge?   Yes ☐   No ☐

27. Please list any institutions with which you have reciprocal arrangements for the free use of other library services.

28. Please give your views on the value and viability of reciprocal arrangements.

29. Can distance learning students from other universities buy external borrower status?

        Yes ☐   No ☐   In some circumstances ☐

        (Please give details)

30. Please give fee categories and amounts for external borrower status

31. To which of the following services do reciprocal arrangements and/or external borrower status give access?
(please tick relevant boxes)

	Reciprocal Arrangement	External Borrower	Additional Charge
Reservations	☐	☐	☐
Borrowing for same periods as your own students	☐	☐	☐
Borrowing for restricted periods or items	☐	☐	☐
Induction to the library	☐	☐	☐
Information skills training	☐	☐	☐
Services of a specialist librarian	☐	☐	☐
Access to OPAC	☐	☐	☐
Use of CD-ROM on stand alone machine	☐	☐	☐
Access to networked databases	☐	☐	☐
Access to BIDS	☐	☐	☐
Inter library loan	☐	☐	☐

32. Do you have an electronic barrier/security system for checking membership on entry?   Yes ☐   No ☐

33. Do you have plans to introduce such a system in the next 12 months?   Yes ☐   No ☐

C. Additional comments regarding library provision for distance learning students.

34. Please use this space to make any additional comments.

Name .... Date: ....

Position ....

Thank you for your help

Please return this questionnaire to: –

The Library in Distance Learning Project, Flexible Learning Centre,
Division of Education, The Education Building, University of Sheffield, Sheffield S10 2JA

APPENDIX 4

Public Library Questionnaire

THE ROLE OF THE LIBRARY IN DISTANCE LEARNING

a research project of the Flexible Learning Centre,
Division of Education, University of Sheffield
funded by the British Library

QUESTIONNAIRE FOR PUBLIC LIBRARIES

Name of Library: ....

Type of library (e.g. central, district, branch): ....

Address: ....

.... Post Code: ....

1. Do your user records separately identify:

	Yes	No		Yes	No
students in general	☐	☐	distance learning students	☐	☐
part-time students	☐	☐	postgraduate distance learning students	☐	☐

2. Have you, or a library in your region, conducted any user surveys which identify **postgraduate distance learning** students and their needs?:   Yes ☐   No ☐   Don't Know ☐

    If yes, please give details: ....

    ....

    ....

3. How extensively is your library used by the following:

	not at all/negligible use	to some extent	extensively	don't know
students in general	☐	☐	☐	☐
part-time students	☐	☐	☐	☐
distance learning students	☐	☐	☐	☐
postgraduate distance learning students	☐	☐	☐	☐

4. Please describe any **formal** involvement of your institution with local HE librarians or networks of HE institutions: ....

    ....

    ....

5. Please describe any specially funded schemes, which may be of benefit to open or distance learning students, with which your library is involved: ....

    ....

    ....

6. Do you offer any of the following to users:

	Yes	No
information about distance learning courses	☐	☐
a collection of distance learning materials	☐	☐
library skills training	☐	☐
training in use of bibliographic resources	☐	☐
specialised literature searches	☐	☐
public access to CD-ROM databases	☐	☐
inter-library loans service	☐	☐

7. Please describe any other training, advice or services which your library can offer which may be of particular value to distance learning students: ....
....
....
....

8. Do you have an on-line public access catalogue (OPAC)?   Yes ☐   No ☐

   If yes, please describe the extent of its coverage (e.g. own library only, county-wide stock): ....
   ....
   ....

9. How adequate would you consider your own stocks of books, journals and bibliographic material for the needs of **postgraduate** distance learning students?

   Completely inadequate ☐   Can provide limited useful material ☐

   Large academic stock ☐   Don't know ☐

10. If you offer an inter-library loans service, how much do you charge per loan? ....

11. Please comment on the level of student use of inter-library loan, and any problems which you have encountered with this service: ....
....
....
....

12. Is an element of your budget reserved to meet the needs of any of these groups?

	Yes	No
students in general	☐	☐
part-time students	☐	☐
distance learning students	☐	☐
postgraduate distance learning students	☐	☐

13. What role, if any, do you think that public libraries should play in support of students following postgraduate distance learning courses? ....
....
....
....

14. Please use this space to add any additional comments regarding the role of public libraries in relation to distance learning: ....
....
....
....
....
....

Name: .... Position: .... Date: ....

Thank you for your help.   Please return this questionnaire to:-
THE LIBRARY IN DISTANCE LEARNING PROJECT, FLEXIBLE LEARNING CENTRE,
DIVISION OF EDUCATION, THE EDUCATION BUILDING, UNIVERSITY OF SHEFFIELD, SHEFFIELD S10 2JA

APPENDIX 5

Student Diary Documents

Library Log: some suggestions for keeping the log

Please complete a 'library log' page each time you make contact with a library, either in person or by any other means.

It does not matter how often you use a library and we are not worried about whether you as an individual are using libraries 'properly'.

If you find you don't really need library access, then that is interesting data for the project.

Use the 'diary notes' part of the sheet to record anything that seems relevant to the project.

This might include:

- Impartial description of events
- Your feelings and reactions to experiences
- Figures, diagrams or pictures
- Details of good services you have come across
- Difficulties in gaining access
- Charges paid
- Good ideas for getting what you need
- Suggestions for improvement of services
- Significant bits of learning about or due to libraries
- Details of remote electronic access using a networked computer

Only use the continuation sheets if you wish to do so.

You could complete the 'personal details' sheet right at the beginning, or at any time during the first 3 months of keeping the diary.

Return your completed library log pages after three months.

LIBRARY LOG: Personal Details

(Please note: Where the information on this sheet is used outside the research team, your anonymity will be protected.)

Name: ....

Address: ....

....

....

Age .... Sex M/F

Occupation... Place of work ....

Number of years in higher education before this course...

Number of years of professional experience ....

Please give the names and addresses of the following libraries so that we can include them in our survey of facilities for distance learning:

Nearest university library to your home or place of work ....

....

....

Names and addresses of the two nearest public libraries.

1. ....　2. ....

....

....

Name and address of any other library which may be important in your study (eg. a work place library)

....

....

....

What experiences of libraries have you had prior to this course, either at work or in education?

....

....

....

What training have you had in library use?

	Current course	*Previous course(s)*
received information pack	☐	☐
guided tour	☐	☐
talk by library staff	☐	☐
library task	☐	☐
hands-on database search	☐	☐
introduction to JANET	☐	☐
course unit or part of unit	☐	☐
other (please describe)	....	....
	....	....
	....	....

LIBRARY LOG

Date:..   Day of week: ....

Please tick the relevant box to show how you made contact with the library:

visit in person	☐
telephone call	☐
contact by post	☐
visit by another person on your behalf	☐
on-line session	☐

Name and location of library ....
....
....

Time spent in, or in contact with, the library: ....

Purpose of using the library: ....
....
....

Services made use of: ....
....
....

Diary notes:

LIBRARY LOG

Date: ....

Diary notes (continuation sheet):

Index